Coping With
An Alcoholic Parent

by
Kay Marie Porterfield

THE ROSEN PUBLISHING GROUP
New York

Published in 1985, 1990 by The Rosen Publishing Group, Inc.
29 East 21st Street, New York, NY 10010

Revised Edition 1990

Library of Congress Cataloging in Publication Data
Porterfield, Kay Marie.
  Coping with an alcoholic parent.

  Includes index.
  Bibliography: p. 136.
  Summary: Suggestions for dealing with alcoholic parents so their drinking doesn't
control their children's feelings and their lives.
    1. Alcoholics—Family relationships.   2. Children of alocholic parents.
[1. Alcoholics—Family relationships.   2. Alcholism]   I. Title.
HV5132.P67   1985   646.7'8   85-14348
ISBN 0-8239-1143-8

Manufactured in the United States of America

Contents

INTRODUCTION

Is This Book for Me?

"My parent is an alcoholic." Those five simple words are frightening to think to yourself, let alone to read or say aloud, aren't they? Even though you've grown far past the stage of believing your parents are perfect, it's not easy to admit that your mother or father may be emotionally and physically dependent on alcohol. In the past perhaps you blamed the arguments at home, the untruths, and the roller-coaster ups and downs on other reasons—perhaps even on yourself. But now you have suspicions that maybe, just maybe, you aren't to blame: The drinking is.

Chances are that you feel a little relieved at that idea and a lot confused. You've heard your parent tell you that he or she can stop drinking anytime. You've seen that your parent hasn't quit. You know that not everyone who drinks is an alcoholic; lots of people drink. But you also know deep inside that there's more to Mom's or Dad's drinking than a couple of beers on Saturday night or a glass of wine with dinner. When you think of alcoholics, you think of bums on the street. Your parent has a job, and your family certainly isn't about to move into a cardboard box in some alley! And aren't alcoholics bad people? Your parent isn't bad. Deciding that Dad or Mom is an alcoholic can feel like calling him or her a dirty name.

Sometimes you may talk yourself out of believing things you've seen with your own eyes and heard with your own ears. Maybe you just imagined the big argument you heard last night after you went to bed. Maybe Dad really does have flu every Monday morning as he tells you, and not a hangover as you suspect. Maybe Mom *is* tired when she comes home from work; maybe she doesn't pass out on the sofa after several drinks before dinner but is taking a nap as she says. Could it be that you're making a big deal out of nothing?

Your doubts are perfectly normal. Alcoholics try to convince themselves and their families that drinking has nothing to do with their problems. Problems are ignored or blamed on other people. If alcoholics admitted they were powerless over alcohol, they'd have to stop drinking. Alcoholics aren't bad people; they are addicted people. They can't imagine living without beer, wine, or liquor, and they deny that drinking is a problem so that they can keep right on doing it. Their addiction blinds them to the truth of what's happening to them and to their families. Kids of alcoholics want to believe what their parents tell them, but they can't ignore what they see and hear. Nobody wants to think a parent isn't telling the truth, so it seems best to keep the confusion inside and to pretend that nothing is wrong.

Things *aren't* right in a home where one parent or both have lost control of drinking. If you aren't sure whether your parent's drinking is causing trouble for you, take a few minutes to read the following statements and on a separate piece of paper keep track of how many you can honestly answer with a yes.

My parent:
- Drinks heavily when he or she is angry, disappointed, nervous, or sad.
- Makes promises to me but doesn't keep them.
- Is drinking more now than he or she used to.
- Hides bottles or sneaks drinks.
- Acts guilty the day after drinking heavily and tries to make up to me for the night before.
- Expects me to take over chores he or she can't do because of drinking.

- Can't remember in the morning what he or she did or said the night before while drinking.
- Becomes nervous when there isn't anything to drink.
- Sometimes blames me for the drinking.
- Gets angry when anyone shows concern about how much he or she drinks.
- Has tried to switch brands or made other rules to cut down on drinking.
- Denies things he or she did while drinking.
- Argues when drunk.
- Often blames me for things I didn't do.
- Eats little or irregularly when drinking.
- Lies about how much he or she has had to drink.
- Always has a "good reason" for drinking.
- Punishes me severely one minute and lets me get away with the same thing the next.
- Can't stop drinking until he or she is drunk.
- Behaves in ways that embarrass me when he or she has been drinking.

I:

- Am ashamed to bring friends home because of the drinking.
- Have a hard time concentrating on schoolwork because my mind is on my parent's drinking.
- Can't make plans because I never know what will happen next depending on how much my parent has had to drink.
- Have tried to hide or get rid of my parent's alcohol.
- Get scared when my parent drinks and argues.
- Try to protect my brothers and sisters when my parent drinks.
- Feel like running away from home to get away from the drinking.
- Wish my parent would quit drinking.

- Sometimes try to pretend the drinking isn't happening.
- Worry about my parent's health because of the drinking.
- Try to hide my parent's drinking from friends and neighbors.
- Feel trapped in the middle between my drinking parent and other people in my family.
- Stay away from home as much as possible to avoid my drinking parent.
- Think if I could just be a better person my parent would stop drinking.
- Feel as though there's no one to talk to about my parent's drinking.
- Always feel angry about my parent's drinking.
- Sometimes think my parents may get divorced because of the drinking.
- Avoid arguments at home at all costs.
- Feel unloved and unwanted when my parent is drinking.
- Get headaches, feel sick to my stomach, or lose sleep when I think about my parent's drinking.

If you answered yes to five or more of those questions, the chances are high that your parent's drinking is out of control. The more questions you answered yes, the more severe that problem is and the more it's affecting *your* life.

Living with an alcoholic parent can be bad news, especially when you understand that there is nothing you can do to *make* your parent stop drinking. Mom or Dad has to come to that decision. Alcoholism is a disease; it can be treated, and many alcoholics recover, but there is no guarantee that your parent will be one of them. The purpose of this book isn't to give you tips on how to persuade Mom or Dad to stop drinking. Such tips probably wouldn't work anyway, and you'd feel angrier and more disappointed than you do already.

The good news is that there *are* ways to stop your parent's drinking from controlling your feelings and your life. You can learn the facts about alcoholism so that you understand why your parent acts the way he or she does. You can find out how a parent's out-of-control drinking affects you and your family in ways you hadn't thought about. You can discover ways to take emotional and physical care of yourself so that you feel better inside and life doesn't seem so crazy and unpredictable. You can find out about people and organizations who are ready and willing to help you.

By reading this book you're making an important first step toward coping with your alcoholic parent. It's a step that many kids in your position will never try. They won't admit that alcohol has become a problem for their parent or that their parent has become a problem for them. They're victims of alcoholism every bit as much as their drinking parents are. Because they refuse to see the problem, they can't hope to find a solution.

You're different. You know what's wrong, and instead of being a victim, you've decided you deserve better. You do! Taking this book from the shelf and opening it took courage. Finishing it will take even more courage, and actually trying the suggestions, the most courage of all. Finding out what you're up against, accepting what you can't change, and working to change the things you can, isn't easy. It *is* worth the effort. *YOU* are worth the effort. You can meet the challenges.

Part 1

IT'S NOT MY FAULT!

CHAPTER I

You Aren't Alone

When your parent is an alcoholic, you often feel very much alone. Except for your brothers and sisters, you probably don't know any other kids who have the same set of problems you do. Even though you may feel alone, you are not alone. An estimated seven million kids under the age of twenty live with at least one alcoholic parent. Children of alcoholics sit with you in English class, live in your neighborhood, and attend your church or synogogue. They are all around you.

Why don't you know about them? For the same reasons they probably haven't guessed that *you* have a problem-drinking parent. Your parent's alcoholism isn't exactly something you want to bring up in a class discussion, and it isn't something you feel like joking about with your friends. Having a parent who drinks too much is no laughing matter. For most kids, it's too embarrassing to talk openly about with friends.

Contrary to popular opinion, most teenagers with an alcoholic parent aren't constantly in trouble. Certainly some kids of alcoholics get bad grades, drink or take drugs, run away, or get arrested. The vast majority go to school and manage to graduate without their teachers, counselors, or friends ever guessing they have a problem. Some choose to have casual rather than close friends so that they never have to invite kids home.

Younger children from alcoholic homes often miss school on Monday mornings. Their clothes may be dirty or mismatched. Many times they're too tired to concentrate, and at recess they may play "drunk." By the time you're a teenager, though, you've learned to take of yourself. You wash your own clothes and you don't play "drunk" anymore. You protect the family secret at all costs because it's frightening to think about what might happen if people found out about your parent's drinking.

Even though they get by, children of alcoholics do have a more difficult time than most. Some are very serious and have no time for fun. Others are perfectionists and are never happy with what they've done. Loneliness is a problem many face. A few have a hard time finishing projects, while others seem driven to finish everything they start even when they no longer want or need to. Some become very upset at surprises, things they can't predict or control.

Obviously, you don't need to have an alcoholic parent to be serious or lonely, lazy or overanxious. Many times children of alcoholics are not noticed because their problems aren't the sort that cause big trouble in school. Few teachers will guess that you didn't turn in your homework because Mom got drunk and ripped it up. Few children of alcoholics will ever admit to outsiders that Mom or Dad drinks too much. Since most kids with an alcoholic parent learn at a very young age not to talk about what's happening at home, few adults or friends find out the truth.

Many kids from alcoholic homes aren't quite sure of the truth themselves. They know they're unhappy, and they suspect something's terribly wrong at home. They guess that drinking might be at the bottom of the trouble, but they can't be certain. After all, their parents deny there's a drinking problem, and they're the adults—they should know. So these kids try to ignore their doubts and pretend that everybody's dad yells with a hangover in the morning or everybody's mom puts cat food in the casserole instead of tuna. Unfortunately, denying a drinking problem doesn't make it go away.

Some counselors call children of alcoholics "invisible victims" because they're so skilled at hiding a parent's drinking problem. Just because they don't announce themselves to the world doesn't mean they don't exist. In every one of your classes there are one or two kids besides you who have a problem drinker for a parent. Who are they?

—Tom, a high school senior, won a basketball scholarship to an out-of-state university, but he has turned it down so he can attend the community college and live at home. There's his mother to think about, and his younger brother and sisters. For the last five years his mother has been drinking steadily. In addition to his studies and practice, Tom cooks meals, cares for the younger children, and tries to keep the house looking neat. At first he shouldered all the work so his dad wouldn't suspect what was happening and get mad. Now his father stays away from home, and Tom has no choice but to act like the head of the household.

He tells himself that his poor housekeeping is the reason he rarely invites his friends home, but the real reason is that he never knows when his mom will embarrass him. Sometimes she doesn't bother to get dressed over weekends, and lately she's been throwing up a lot. Besides, he doesn't have time to socialize. It's not so bad when she's at work, but evenings are tough. When she drinks scotch and cries, he feels responsible for her sadness and he worries that she might be going crazy. Part of him wants to walk out the front door and leave for good, but he has a duty to make sure she doesn't do something bad to herself. If he moved, who would pack the younger kids' lunches and write their notes for school?

—Michelle, a tenth grader, can't wait until she's sixteen and can quit school. The teachers are just like her dad—real creeps. Most of the time he doesn't pay much attention to her at all. He's too busy working as the director of an ad agency.

For as long as she can remember, he's worked late and staggered home drunk. Some nights he forgets to come home. When he remembers, he gets furious and hits Michelle's mother. He blames both his wife and his daughter for forcing him to work so hard and to drink because of his rough days at work. Michelle can't do homework or even sleep with all the yelling and screaming going on. Many mornings she's too tired to bother going to school, but that's no problem because her mom calls and says she doesn't feel well.

Of course, after Dad has sobered up, he feels guilty and hands Michelle and her mom a couple of hundred-dollar bills and tells them to go shopping. Michelle is sick of the whole routine and mad at her father. All he thinks about is success and his next drink. She's *never* going to be like him even if it means dropping out of school and marrying her boyfriend, whom her father can't stand. She's thought about trying to get help, but who would believe her? Sometimes she thinks the only solution is to run away.

—Sean, a seventh grader, dreads his twice-monthly visits with his father. In the beginning, right after the divorce, Dad drank a lot but was fun to be around. The jokes and the silliness made the weekends seem like parties. Now Dad is drinking more, and he's crabby most of the time. When Sean gets upset with frequently changed plans and broken promises, his father grouches even more and insists that he doesn't have a drinking problem: He can't, because he only drinks beer.

Lately though, Sean has stopped believing him. There's rarely any food in the house, and Dad often forgets about meals entirely. At night when Sean is in bed, his father goes out to bars for a "couple of beers" and stays away for hours at a time. Riding in the car with him after he's downed a six-pack is terrifying. Torn between loyalty to his dad and the unpleasant visits, Sean copes by staying in his room and listening to the radio for hours at a time. Avoiding his father when he's been drinking and when he has hangovers is boring, but it's a way to survive. Sean sees his dad becoming a different person, one who is *very* hard to love. Still if he tells anyone, especially his mom, he's afraid he'll never be able to see his father again, so he keeps his mouth shut and his head phones on.

Maybe you can recognize bits and pieces of yourself in the descriptions of Tom, Michelle, and Sean. Then again, maybe you can't. That's not unusual. Kids of alcoholics have a lot of things in common, but they have differences, too. They aren't like so many cookies cut with the same cookie cutter. They are unique individuals. *You* are a unique individual.

While most teens with a problem-drinking parent share some of the fear, anger, and sad helplessness that Tom, Michelle, and Sean carry inside, not everyone feels those exact emotions or feels them with the same intensity. Even though you may have some of the same experiences as those one or two other kids of alcoholics who sit in your history or English class, other experiences will be different. Some of the things you read about in this book will fit your life and some won't.

How Family Alcoholism Affects You
Depends on Many Things:

—At what point in your life did your parent's problem drinking begin? Some teens have memories of life before a parent's alcoholism, while others can't remember when their parent didn't abuse alcohol. If you can recall a time when Mom or Dad didn't get drunk and when life at home was happier than it is now, you may feel very sad or bitter about your present circumstances, but you know things can change. On the other hand, if all you've known is a parent with a drinking problem, you may doubt that things can ever get better. Because you've never lived a "normal" life, you might not be clear about what you're aiming for now. What's normal?

—How severe is your parent's drinking problem? As the disease of alcoholism progresses, your parent's behavior will change. Parents in the early stages of alcoholism may forget things, drive when drunk, and be irritable or depressed; but they still go to work and make some effort, even if it is a small one, to do their jobs around the house. As time passes an alcoholic parent will drink more and more and may tremble or see things that aren't there. Instead of being absent-minded, problem-drinking parents at this stage have blackouts and aren't aware of their actions for big chunks of time. It becomes impossible for them to hold jobs or even to pretend to act like parents. As the alcoholism gets worse, the good times become further and further apart. The more severe your parent's alcohol problem, the more it affects you.

—When and where does your parent drink? Some alcoholics are binge drinkers. They don't drink most of the time but every so often drink uncontrollably for a few days or even months. In between those drinking bouts, things may run pretty smoothly, except that everyone is dreading the next period of drunkenness. Other alcoholics drink chronically; that is, most of the time. Their families live constantly with their drinking and out-of-control behavior. If your parent drinks mostly at bars or parties and away from home, your problems and feelings won't be quite the same as a teenager who must watch Mom or Dad drink to the point of passing out nearly every night. In fact you may have only recently connected the slurred speech and the stumbling to your parent's drinking.

—How does your parent act when he or she has been drinking? Not all alcoholics behave the same way when they drink. Some are loud and silly—the life of the party. Others grow depressed; they may cry and talk about taking their lives. Many are easily irritated and blow their tops for no reason. You won't have the same reaction to a parent who drinks quietly until he or she passes out as you will to a parent who drinks, picks fights, and then yells at you. Whether you feel embarrassment, fear, anger, or worry is based in part on your parent's drinking behavior.

—How much trouble has your parent's drinking caused your family and you? Some families seem to keep going in spite of a parent's problem drinking. Others fall apart. The divorce rate for alcoholics is eleven times higher than it is for other people. When alcoholism affects a parent's ability to work, money can be a big problem. Divorce and money troubles make life doubly difficult for kids of alcoholics. Accidents, illness, and frequent moves are other upsets that can be triggered by a parent's drinking problem. As a general rule, the bigger the changes your parent's drinking has caused for you and for your family, the more you'll be upset by the drinking.

—How old are you? The older you are, the more able you are to protect yourself against some of the problems your parent's drinking causes you. When Mom "forgets" to fix dinner or Dad passes out on the living room floor, all a little kid can do is cry. You can fix a sandwich and go read a book or take a walk. One of the good things about growing up is that you are better able to take care of yourself. The bad part of it is that you may have to take care of younger brothers and sisters. That can be a full-time job, and it hurts to miss out on the fun other kids are having.

—Do you have someone you can talk with? Sometimes you can talk to your nonalcoholic parent, but not always. Some kids have *two* alcoholic parents. Others have a nonalcoholic parent who is caught up in protecting a problem-drinking husband or wife. Some husbands and wives are so hurt and bitter about the alcohol problem that they don't want to talk. It isn't always easy to find people who will listen to a teenager with an alcoholic parent. Neighbors and old family friends may not want to get involved, and you may be too shy to talk to a teacher or a coach. Making close friends and having to worry what they'll think when they find out the truth can be scary, too.

Everyone needs a support network, people to talk with and hang out with. Aunts and uncles, grandparents, neighbors, friends, teachers—all can be part of your support network. They are your safety net for times when things get rough at home. Research shows that children of alcoholics who have relationships outside their home usually survive the situation in good shape.

Not all children of alcoholics are alike, not all alcoholics are alike, and not all families are alike. Even so, kids of alcoholics do have many things in common besides a parent with a drinking problem. Lots of kids carry around quite a few wrong ideas about just what having an alcoholic parent means.

Myths and Facts about Kids of Alcoholics and Their Parents:

MYTH: Living with an alcoholic parent will ruin my life forever.

FACT: Absolutely not! Research shows that not all kids of alcoholics are affected to the same degree. Some manage to grow up with little or no emotional harm. It is true that having an alcoholic parent may make it harder for you to live a happy and well-adjusted life now and when you grow up, but it doesn't make it impossible. Remember, you have a good deal of say as to whether or not your life will be "ruined." Feeling hopeless, helpless, and doomed won't do you any good.

MYTH: My alcoholic parent has a problem; I don't.

FACT: Alcoholism is a family disease. Even though you aren't addicted to alcohol, you are hooked on your parent's drinking problem. If you ever feel angry about your parent's drinking, sad about broken promises, or frightened about what will happen to your parent, you have a problem. If you find yourself thinking and worrying about your parent's drinking, you have a problem. When drinking controls your parent, your parent's unpredictable actions definitely affect your life. You can't solve your parent's problem, but you can solve yours.

MYTH: Having an alcoholic mother is worse for a kid than having an alcoholic father.

FACT: Research doesn't support that idea, even though having an alcoholic mother may seem worse to you. Society doesn't approve when a woman becomes an alcoholic: Alcoholic women aren't shy and quiet; they don't act in ways women are expected to behave. At the same time, those same people often tacitly approve of a man who drinks too much and think he's acting macho. There's a double standard for men and women. Studies show that fathers are more important to kids than we used to think. Having either an alcoholic mother or an alcoholic father makes life difficult.

MYTH: If my parent stopped drinking, everything would be fine.

FACT: If your parent stopped drinking, certainly your life would improve, but it is unrealistic to think that all of your problems would vanish immediately. Blaming everything that's wrong from acne to poor grades on your parent's drinking is a way to avoid responsibility for solving your own problems. When you blame, you give your parent and the drinking problem total control over your life.

MYTH: My parent who doesn't have an alcohol problem ought to listen to me and help me.

FACT: Remember, alcoholism is a family disease. That means both of your parents are affected even though only one drinks. Many nonalcoholic parents spend most of their time trying to keep the alcoholic from drinking and covering for that parent when drinking happens. There may not be much time left over to listen to your concerns. Bitterness, disappointment, and anger can get in the way of parenting, too. Some nonalcoholic parents deny there's a drinking problem just as strongly as does the alcoholic. How much your other parent can help you depends on how "hooked" into the spouse's alcohol problem he or she is.

MYTH: My alcoholic parent is a terrible person.

FACT: Alcoholism is a disease. Your parent didn't decide to be an alcoholic. Alcoholism is sneaky; it creeps up on people. They start out wanting a drink and end up needing one. By the time a parent is alcohol-dependent, denial has set in, and it is very difficult to admit to a drinking problem and to seek treatment. That would mean giving up alcohol.

MYTH: My alcoholic parent doesn't love me.

FACT: Alcoholics, because they are emotionally and physically addicted, put alcohol ahead of everything else in their lives—including you. They still care about you deep inside. Most alcoholic parents love their children very much, but when they are drinking they may do and say some pretty awful things. That's part of the disease, too. Don't take it personally.

MYTH: Kids of alcoholics drive their parents to drink.

FACT: No one can force another person to drink. Alcohol-dependent parents think they can cope with stress by drinking. Often their heavy drinking starts during your teenage years, so you may feel as if your growing pains have driven them to drink. Your problem-drinking parent might even blame you for his or her drinking. Don't buy it. Blame, remember, is a way to avoid responsibility for solving our own problems. Alcoholics are experts at blaming their troubles on everything and everyone except alcohol.

MYTH: Nice families don't have problems with alcohol.

FACT: Alcoholism cuts across all races and income levels. One out of every ten drinkers in the U.S. is an alcoholic, and few of them are bag ladies or hobos. In fact, three fourths of all drinking alcoholics have jobs and families. Alcoholics don't always get into trouble with the law because of their drinking and, as we've said before, only a few children of alcoholics are troublemakers. The idea that you have to be poverty-stricken, a bum, or a criminal to be affected by alcoholism just isn't true.

MYTH: Most alcoholics beat, neglect, or sexually abuse their kids.

FACT: Some do. Most don't. The rate of neglect and abuse is higher in homes where one parent or both are alcoholic. But just because your parent has a drinking problem doesn't mean that terrible things will happen to you. Alcohol lowers inhibitions, but it does not *make* people act violently. If you feel in danger of physical or sexual abuse, you can take steps to protect yourself (see Chapter VII).

MYTH: Alcoholics can't get well.

FACT: They can, and many of them do. You may have heard or read that there's no "cure" for alcoholism, and that can seem pretty grim. There is no cure in the sense that an alcoholic can never drink normally. The alcoholism doesn't disappear, but it can be treated. When an alcoholic stops drinking, he or she can live a happy and productive life.

Quite a few alcoholics seek treatment, stop drinking, and put their lives back on track. This is especially true for alcohol-dependent people who still have jobs and families. You can't force your parent to get help, but you can work on your own problems and get help for yourself. Often when one person in a family changes for the better, other family members do, too. As you read this book you'll learn more about how to make the changes you need to make within yourself.

CHAPTER II

Alcoholism: The Facts

Alcohol is a drug, just as barbiturates and tranquilizers are drugs. It is a mood-altering substance, a potent depressant of the central nervous system, or "downer." But unlike most other drugs, alcohol doesn't require a prescription and it is legal—at least for adults. People of drinking age can buy beer, wine, and distilled spirits at liquor and grocery stores. Almost every town, large and small, boasts a number of nightclubs and bars where liquor is sold by the drink.

Americans drink at parties and family gatherings. They drink to celebrate, to forget their troubles, and to unwind after a hard day at work. From every side we are bombarded with the idea that drinking is the sexy and friendly thing to do. In fact about 100 million, or two thirds, of the people in this country drink alcohol regularly. Because so many Americans use alcohol, it's easy to forget that the chemical is a powerful sedative and that people can and do become addicted to it.

What Does Alcohol Do?

What does alcohol do when someone, anyone, drinks it? Let's take a look at Fred. He's a thirty-six-year-old insurance salesman and school board member who rarely drinks. When he does, he has only a glass or two of wine with his dinner. This year at his birthday party, however, he pulled out all the stops and drank far too much. Fred told himself the rum punch was mostly fruit juice, so it was harmless; he could drink as much as he wanted.

After two drinks in a hour's time, alcohol began to affect Fred's judgment. He felt uninhibited, silly, lightheaded, very relaxed, and willing to take bigger risks than usual. A normally serious person, he started telling off-color jokes and tried to stand on his hands, to the embarrassment of his teenage son, John. Even small amounts of alcohol decrease a person's ability to taste and smell, and Fred was no exception. The potato chips tasted like cardboard to him, so he started salting them. That made him thirstier, and he made his way to the punch bowl again.

After two more drinks, alcohol started to affect the part of Fred's brain that controls coordination. He became clumsy and stumbled, dropped an ashtray, and talked with slurred speech. Even though he could still see clearly, he developed "tunnel vision" and didn't notice objects on either side of him. His reaction time slowed, so it would have been dangerous for him to drive or operate machinery. After he caught his tie in the electric can opener, he decided on another glass of punch to celebrate his escape.

That was the drink that made Fred officially drunk. The brain centers that controlled his coordination were severely affected. Stumbling turned into staggering, and he had great difficulty moving. After he banged his shins on the coffee table and overturned it, all he wanted to do was lie down. Still, he had to think of his guests, so with great effort he stood up again. At this stage alcohol also had started to affect Fred's emotions. His laughter was far too loud, and when his wife mentioned it, he grew angry and argued with her. His lack of inhibitions meant that he saw nothing wrong with swearing at her within earshot of company. Other drinkers might start to cry uncontrollably or act foolishly after drinking this much.

After he had downed several more drinks, Fred had trouble paying attention to what was going on around him. He couldn't understand what he saw or heard and became confused. Because moving was difficult for him now, he lay down on the sofa and stared blankly as his guests began to leave. After a final glass of punch, Fred passed out and began to snore. Even though he had made a fool of himself and both his wife and son were furious with him, he was lucky. Occasionally the concentration of alcohol in a drinker's system is so high that it blocks the brain centers that instruct the lungs to breathe and the heart to beat. When that happens the drinker dies. Another word for being drunk is intoxicated. That "toxic" in the middle isn't there by accident: In large amounts, alcohol is poisonous.

Because alcohol *is* a drug, it is especially dangerous in combination with other drugs such as sleeping pills, pain killers, cold remedies, and tranquilizers. Since they act on the same parts of the brain as do beer, wine, or liquor, these medications have a profound impact on the central nervous system. Their effects don't merely add to alcohol's effects, they *multiply* them. Had Fred been taking medicine, he would have raced through the stages of intoxication.

Even though many people receive the impression from advertisements and television shows that alcohol is glamorous, what happens when a person drinks isn't pretty. If your mother or father drinks too much, you know that already. Maybe you didn't know that getting drunk is the very same thing that happens when a person takes too many sedatives, barbiturates, or ether, an anesthetic. Not so long ago, doctors used alcohol to make patients unconscious during surgery. No wonder when someone gets drunk we say they're feeling no pain!

Often, sobering up the next morning is the real pain for drinkers. Because alcohol disturbs sleep patterns, Fred didn't reach the deep dream stage of sleep, and he woke up feeling tired, grouchy, and nervous. His face was green as he sat at the breakfast table and growled at John not to bother him. The morning after drinking to excess, it's common have a pounding headache and feel sick. Fred threw up and spent the day in bed, vowing never to drink so much again. He'd learned his lesson.

Problem Drinker or Alcoholic?

Of all the people who drink, most of them drink to excess only a few times before they "wise up" and drink moderately or not at all. A third of Americans over fourteen years old drink once a year or less. Another third, the light drinkers, average a little over one drink a week. A quarter of Americans are moderate drinkers who have up to one drink a day. Only one out of every nine to ten drinkers consumes more than that. Some drink *much* more. A third of the people in this country buy and drink 90 percent of all the alcohol sold. Alcohol plays a very big part in their lives and the lives of the people who live with them. Many of these heavy drinkers are problem drinkers and alcoholics.

Both terms, problem drinker and alcoholic, are words you'll be reading often in the chapters to come. If they are confusing to you, don't feel bad; even scientists are often mixed up about them. Many experts believe that problem drinking and alcoholism are different. They say that a problem drinker is a person who drinks to cope, gets drunk often, and whose drinking causes problems with his or her work or marriage. An alcoholic, on the other hand, has a physical craving for and dependency on alcohol.

People with the disease alcoholism have no control over their drinking because their bodies handle alcohol differently than those of normal people. Problem drinkers may learn to control their drinking by consuming only small amounts of alcohol and then stopping. Alcoholics, however, must stop drinking completely if they are to get well.

In real life, it is almost impossible to tell problem drinkers from alcoholics. Problem drinkers as well as alcoholics will tell you they can quit any time. More often than not, they don't. Many problem drinkers who start drinking to cope with life eventually become alcoholics whose bodies crave booze in order to function. Both drink to the point of drunkenness. Both allow their drinking to make trouble for themselves and their families.

Even the alcohol experts have trouble deciding who is an alcoholic and who is a problem drinker. It's not so much a matter of how much a person drinks, but how often, when, and why. You have no real way of knowing whether your mom or dad drinks too much because of outside stresses or because of what his or her body does to alcohol. In fact, the only sure way to tell whether a person is a problem drinker or an alcoholic is to administer complicated medical tests. In the meantime, alcohol is the central focus in the lives of both types of drinkers. Whether their alcohol dependence is mental or physical, its effects aren't pleasant.

When your mom is drunk and forgets to pick you up from school, or your dad drinks so much that he yells at you when you haven't done anything wrong, you are hurt by their alcohol consumption whether it's problem drinking or alcoholism. If you're angry, sad, or frightened about a parent's drinking, labels don't mean much to you but your unpleasant feelings do. The bad things happening in your life are more important than labels. Sometimes in this book we use "problem drinker" and "alcoholic" to mean the same thing, because alcoholics and problem drinkers have a lot in common: They are people whose drinking causes problems for themselves and for those around them.

Alcoholics and problem drinkers both abuse the drug alcohol, and alcohol *abuse* is a serious problem. Just how serious?

—Drunk driving is involved in over half of all highway deaths. It is the leading cause of death for people aged fifteen to twenty-four.

—Two out of every five people will be involved in an alcohol-related crash during their lives.

—Drinking is involved in 45 to 68 percent of cases of spouse abuse and 38 percent of child abuse.

—Fetal alcohol syndrome, caused when pregnant women drink, is the third leading cause of mental retardation.

—Alcoholism and problem drinking kill 97,000 people a year from cirrhosis of the liver and other illnesses, mental illness, murder, suicide, and accident.

—Alcohol-related accidents, medical costs, violent crimes, and days lost at work cost almost $117,000 billion a year.

—One out of every four U.S. households is affected by alcoholism.

—Although alcoholism is our second leading disease next to heart disease, people donate only about 15 cents per alcoholic for research and treatment.

—Alcohol abuse is our biggest drug problem both in scope and in destructiveness.

These facts are not comforting. Learning that alcohol is a drug and that your alcoholic parent has a drug problem can seem like a nightmare come true. Finding out that untreated alcoholism causes so many problems and can even be fatal is frightening. Even though facing up to the facts about uncontrolled drinking isn't easy, you need to know what you're up against before you can take steps to make *your* life better.

Alcoholism is a treatable illness, and when alcoholics are treated the recovery rate is high. Before an alcoholic or family members will reach out for help, they must know that alcoholism is a serious problem. Pretending that alcoholism is no big deal or ignoring it doesn't make it go away; it only makes things worse.

Why My Parent?

Right now, you're probably wondering why, when 90 million people drink alcohol without becoming addicted, *your* mom or dad isn't one of them. Why does your mother drink until she passes out or your father drive under the influence? Why do you have to make excuses and feel ashamed when you bring friends home? It's not fair!

You're right. It *isn't* fair, and neither are the answers to your questions simple. No one knows exactly why some people become alcoholics while others don't. Two things are absolutely certain. First, your parent's drinking problem is *not* your fault.

Second, your parent's alcoholism isn't his or her fault either. Alcoholism is a disease, as is diabetes or high blood pressure. Certainly, if Mom or Dad had never taken that first drink, there wouldn't be, a drinking problem today. Unfortunately your parent didn't know then that he or she would become addicted to alcohol.

Accepting that alcoholism is not anyone's "fault" isn't the same as feeling good about the disease. You have every right to be angry at the unfairness of alcoholism, at your parent's behavior, and at the decision not to seek treatment. But condemning your parent for having the disease in the first place is a different matter. You may feel better for a little while, but finger-pointing doesn't help you to cope with your parent's drinking problem. Understanding *can* help you cope.

While we don't know precisely what causes alcoholism, we do have some clues. For instance, we know it strikes young people, adults, and the elderly. Women can be alcoholic just as men can. Although some ethnic groups seem more prone to alcoholism than others, alcoholics come from all racial groups and ethnic backgrounds. Some people can drink heavily for twenty years or so before they become physically addicted to alcohol, whereas for others addiction happens within a space of days or months.

Since alcoholism isn't caused by germs, it isn't "catching." Some alcoholics started out by being problem drinkers who drank and drank until they became addicted. Perhaps they drank heavily to escape their troubles. Perhaps they saw their parents drink to "solve" problems and imitated them, or they drank to fit in with their friends. At this point they became psychologically dependent on drinking. Because they felt liked, happy, and carefree when they drank, they thought they couldn't get by without booze. Gradually their bodies crossed the line from alcohol abuse to alcohol addiction without their knowing what was happening.

Some alcoholics seem to develop the disease by drinking too much over a long period of time because of social pressures or to cope with stress. After using alcohol as an emotional crutch, they find they can't stop drinking.

Other people seem to have been born with a predisposition to alcohol. That means that something about their physical makeup makes them more likely to develop alcoholism than are other people. Their bodies metabolize (break down) alcohol differently than most people's do. Many scientists believe that this predisposition is inherited; that is, handed down from parents and grandparents like brown eyes or curly hair. And, yes, such a predisposition can be passed on to you. We'll talk about that in a later chapter.

We know that alcohol itself doesn't turn people into alcoholics. Neither do mental problems make people alcoholic. While some people drink to forget their emotional troubles and then get caught up in addiction, not all people do. Addiction happens because of what goes on inside a drinker's body, not what goes on inside a drinker's head. Alcoholics aren't crazy, even though at times they may act that way.

In recent years researchers have found several things that make alcoholics different from other people. When alcoholics drink, they go through the same stages Fred did, with some very important extras. These extras have nothing to do with moral weakness or personality defects. Instead they are part of an alcoholic's physical makeup and brain chemistry.

The first of these differences is a preference for alcohol. Given a choice between milk, coffee, or juice and a beer, alcoholics will pick the beer. Why? Because alcohol in all its forms tastes better to alcoholics than to other people. In fact, alcoholics like both the taste and the effects of alcohol so much that they drink nearly every chance they get and they drink until they pass out.

Scientists have found that mice are like people when it comes to liking or disliking alcohol: Some avoid it, and others drink as much as possible. Researchers were able to breed and raise a family of mice that chose alcohol over water nearly every time, just as alcoholics do.

When they analyzed the brains of these mice, they found a significant difference between them and the ones that drank moderately or not at all. The "alcoholic" animals are born unable to manufacture as much of a brain chemical called endorphin as the normal mice.

Endorphin is present in everyone's brain to some extent. It makes us feel content and happy as well as dulling physical pain; it is a natural opiate or sedative. When mice or humans cannot make as much endorphin as they need, they seek out other sedatives, which are provided by drugs or drinking.

One researcher discovered that most people can't recall the first time they ever took a drink. If they do remember the experience, they don't think it was a pleasant one; the alcohol didn't taste very good to them. Alcoholics, on the other hand, have sharp memories of their first drink and say that it made them feel good. Alcoholics and nonalcoholics have two very different ways of thinking about drinking, from the very first drink. It's as if alcoholics, when they drink, find a missing part of themselves that they've lacked from birth. That piece may be endorphin.

Not every alcoholic or problem drinker is born without the ability to make enough natural endorphin. Some people, maybe your mom or dad, started drinking because of a stressful situation. It could have been the loss of a job or divorce or simple shyness at parties. Heavy drinking, for whatever reason, diminishes the ability to make endorphin. Even if people make enough in the first place, after a period of heavy drinking they need more. The more these people drink to feel good, the more they need to drink before they start feeling good! After a while they are addicted to alcohol every bit as much as people who were born with an endorphin deficiency.

Another difference between alcoholics and other drinkers is in the way their bodies break down the alcohol. When most people drink beer, wine, or liquor, their bodies eliminate it at the rate of about one drink an hour. First the alcohol is changed into acetaldehyde. Acetaldehyde is a poison, but the liver quickly breaks it down into acetic acid (vinegar) and then, after more steps, into water and carbon dioxide, which the kidneys and lungs eliminate.

The alcoholic's body, however, retains a tiny bit of acetaldehyde. It travels to the brain, where it's turned into something you'd never want to meet on a spelling test: tetrahydroisoquinoline, or THIQ for short. THIQ is closely related to heroin, and it is very addictive. During World War II, medical researchers decided it couldn't be used as a painkiller because people became addicted to it more quickly than they did to morphine. Considering that only alcoholic drinkers, and not normal drinkers, make THIQ, you can understand why alcohol is so important to your parent.

Returning to the alcoholic and the nondrinking mice, the ones who don't like alcohol won't touch it unless the researchers give them a tiny shot of THIQ. Then the nondrinking mice can't get enough alcohol; they become alcoholic drinkers. Animal studies also show that once THIQ is in the brain, it doesn't disappear even when the animal isn't given alcohol. That explains why some alcoholics stop drinking for many years and suddenly take up right where they left off. It also explains why the only effective way to treat physical alcohol addiction is for the alcoholic to stop drinking entirely. With a brain full of THIQ, it's impossible to stop at just one drink.

Alcoholics also seem to tolerate alcohol better than other people. Their bodies adapt more quickly and completely to alcohol's upsetting effects than the bodies of normal drinkers. Most people drink moderately or not at all because booze leaves them feeling tired, dizzy, and nauseated. But even before an alcoholic begins drinking a lot—in fact, while drinking the same amount as a normal drinker—the alcoholic's brain cells are changing so that they function well when alcohol is present. At this stage, alcoholics can outdrink their friends and not seem drunk. Who would guess that people who can hold their liquor that well have a problem? But they do have a problem. The process of physical addiction to alcohol has begun.

Before long and without warning, the cells have adapted to alcohol so well that they don't function very well without it. When alcoholics don't get enough to drink, they feel awful. Because they are physically addicted to alcohol, they need it constantly. That's why Dad may have to have a drink in the morning before he brushes his teeth or why Mom hides a bottle in the kitchen cupboard and sneaks drinks all day long.

Many alcoholics do what is called maintenance drinking. If they don't take a drink every few minutes their hands start to shake and they may see things that aren't there. Yet even though alcohol makes them feel normal, it is destroying their brain and liver cells. Most alcoholics don't know this because they feel sickest, not when they drink, but when they *don't* drink.

The things we've been talking about are complicated, but maybe they've made it easier for you to understand that alcoholism is not a disease your parent chose to get. Whether alcoholics are born with a chemical deficiency or drink until their body chemistry changes, their alcoholism isn't purposeful. It is a very real disease.

As we told you, it also runs in families. About half of all alcoholics have an alcoholic parent. If you count uncles, aunts, brothers, and cousins, more than nine out of ten alcoholics have relatives who are addicted to alcohol. Research also shows that children who are separated from their alcoholic parent or parents at birth and raised by nonalcoholics have a four to five times greater risk of becoming alcoholic than other kids. Because they didn't learn alcoholic drinking patterns from their adoptive parents, the chances are that their alcoholism was handed down genetically from their real parents. Other studies show that children of alcoholics and brothers and sisters of alcoholics are affected more strongly by alcohol than other people are.

We call alcoholism a "family disease" for another reason, too. It is different from diabetes and other inherited diseases in one important way. If your mother or father were diabetic, he or she would have health problems from eating the wrong foods. Unless you had diabetes, too, you would feel very bad about your parent's choice to ignore the disease, but you could at least live your life normally.

It's not quite the same for alcoholic families. When parents drink, they don't quietly become ill. They break promises, throw temper tantrums, or become depressed. They embarrass you in front of your friends and make your life frightening and uncertain. Your parents' problem becomes *your* problem when their drunkenness controls your life.

Part 2

HEY, WHAT'S GOING ON HERE?
LIVING IN AN ALCOHOLIC HOME

CHAPTER III

Problems at Home

—Cynthia told her mother three weeks ago that she needed a dress for the Senior Class Dance. Everyone would be wearing long gowns, and she didn't have one. Her mother promised to take her shopping, but every evening she was too intoxicated to drive, and on weekend mornings when she wasn't drunk, she was too tired. Two days before the dance, she told her daughter they couldn't afford a dress; their money must be spent for important things. "Like booze?" Cynthia countered. "You spend at least forty dollars a week on that!"

—When Bob came home from school and turned on his stereo, his father burst into the room and smashed it. "I've told you and told you, I hate that loud music," he yelled. The truth was that Bob's dad griped about the music sometimes, but often he liked to listen to it, too. It all depended on how much he'd had to drink, which was hard for Bob to know. His dad had even told him how proud he was that Bob had earned the money for the system himself. As he looked at the parts that lay scattered about the room, broken beyond repair, Bob was so angry he wanted to lash out and strike his father.

—Megan's parents were fighting again. With a frown, she put her hands over her ears and tried to concentrate on her history book. But she couldn't blot out the sounds coming from the living room—the thumps and bumps and accusations. Both Mom and Dad had been drinking heavily, and lately more and more evenings were filled with loud arguing. It was useless to try and study for tomorrow's test! She slammed the book shut and tearfully wondered how much longer she could get passing grades when her family was falling apart around her.

Even though Cynthia, Bob, and Megan don't drink, they all have an alcoholism problem because they have alcoholic parents. The physical changes that take place in an alcoholic's body are only part of the disease. Both problem drinkers and alcoholics behave very differently from other people. They break promises, they are unpredictable, and they have trouble getting along with people. Alcohol is the most important thing in their lives—even more important than their kids.

It may hurt you to read that, but it is true. Even though you may not have thought about it before, more than likely deep inside you've felt cheated and left out sometimes. Alcohol is a drug, and alcoholism is an addiction. Chemically dependent people, no matter what their drug, feel they cannot live without it. Their lives are centered on finding the drug, taking the drug, and hiding their addiction so that no one will find out about it and make them stop. This takes so much time and energy that there's little left for being a parent.

Cynthia's mom wasn't being mean when she broke promises to buy her daughter a dress. She truly believed that the dress wasn't nearly as important as the vodka she couldn't get through the day without. Bob's dad loved his son, but his drinking affected his emotions and his memory so that it was impossible for him to act logically after he'd had two six-packs of beer. It never crossed Megan's parents' minds that their drinking and fighting were affecting her grades. Usually they'd forgotten about their battles by the next morning.

Most problem-drinking and alcoholic parents aren't completely awful. They have their good days and their bad ones. Just as alcoholic families have a lot of pain, anger, and fear, they have moments of caring and happiness, too. But because drinking is the most important thing to alcoholic parents and because alcohol affects their emotions and behavior, they can't give you all the things you need for a happy childhood and adolescence.

Sure, you may have food and clothes, a place to live and an allowance, but we're talking about the things you can't see, things that are every bit as important to you as peanut butter and sweatshirts—maybe even more important. Those needs are *love, security, acceptance, control, guidance, independence,* and *faith.*

No parent, even a parent who doesn't drink, can do a perfect job of providing those things for you. And very few parents, even alcoholic parents, fail to give their kids any of them. Alcoholic and problem-drinking mothers and fathers do have an especially hard time meeting your needs because they are so wrapped up in themselves and their drinking.

Where does that leave you? To find out, let's use that basic list of things you need and talk about each item. As you read, keep in mind that not all alcoholics are alike, not all families are alike, and certainly not all teenagers are alike. Some of the things we talk about may not apply to you and your parents at all, but chances are that some of them do.

Love. Most parents love their children, and alcoholic or problem-drinking parents are no exception. Chemically dependent parents have trouble letting you know that they love you. Even when a drinking parent gives a lot of hugs, kisses, and words of praise, the kids are no dummies: They can figure out that alcohol is number one in their parent's life. It hurts to know you're number two when there's nothing you can do about it.

Depending on how much your parent has had to drink and on how alcohol affects your parent's emotions, he or she can say and do some pretty terrible things. When Brad gets home from junior high where he's an eighth grader, his mom is usually lounging by the pool, drink in hand. She asks him how his day has gone, and even though she's acting silly, she smiles and laughs a lot. If only she would stay that way, but she doesn't. By dinnertime, she's had much more to drink, and she's grouchy. Because Brad's father often works late, she takes her frustrations out on her son. "If it hadn't been for you, I could have gone to graduate school and I'd have a good job now," she tells him with tears in her eyes. "I'd be independent and I could divorce the jerk. Why were you ever born?"

Brad wonders the same thing, but it's too late to do anything about it now! Like many children of alcoholics, he gets mixed messages. One minute his mom acts as if she loves him and the next minute as if she doesn't. What is he supposed to believe?

When parents are drunk, they have little or no control over what they say or do. Even though the emotions they feel may have little to do with their kids, it doesn't come out that way. Whether parents are screaming in anger or feeling sorry for themselves, it is hard to believe they love you when they blame their bad feelings on you.

In the beginning stages of alcoholism, your parent may have pushed you aside only when drinking, but as the disease continues you are pushed away more often and your feelings of being unloved may grow. That's because addicted drinkers don't have time to care for other people; they're always concerned with drinking.

Security. You need to know your home is a safe place, that you won't be hurt there either emotionally or physically. Even though you're a teenager and can take care of yourself better than when you were a little kid, it's good to know that an adult is around and willing to help you out of difficulties. You want to count on your parents to be there when you need them and to keep their word. Alcoholic and problem-drinking parents not only are gone when you need them during a crisis, but often they *cause* the crisis.

Shauna's father rarely drinks at home; instead he drinks at bars and with his friends. When he first started drinking heavily, he would spend the night away from his family. Because Shauna's mother worked nights, the teenager was often alone and responsible for her younger brothers and sisters. "It was scary," she says, "I was only thirteen, and it was like I was the head of the family. I'd get so worried I couldn't sleep nights."

Lately, Shauna's dad stays out drinking for days at a time. He's lot his job, so money is a big worry. But more important to Shauna, he loses his temper when he does stagger home. After picking a fight with her, it isn't unusual for him to throw her clothes out the front door and kick her out of the house because he doesn't like her friends or the way she dresses. Although her mother calms him down and talks him into taking her back, Shauna is sure that one day he'll make her leave home for good. That's an extremely frightening thought for a fifteen-year-old.

In the middle and later stages of alcoholism, people with the disease become fearful that they'll lose their jobs. Sometimes the worst happens and they are fired. When that happens, families worry about how to pay the bills. Many times relatives and old friends are put off by the drinking and aren't around to help. Feeling that it's you and your family against the world is scary.

While not all alcoholic and problem-drinking parents beat their children, some do lose control. How can you feel secure when you have an angry parent who hits you or threatens to hurt you? Neglect may be a problem for you if your parents drink and go off forgetting that they have a family. You, like Shauna, may have to take responsibility for younger brothers and sisters before you're really old enough to do that.

Finally, divorce can be a big problem for kids with an alcoholic parent or parents. Because alcoholics and problem drinkers have a hard time getting along with people, it isn't always easy for them to stay married. When they do manage to keep their relationship together, frequently they argue. If you hear your parents fighting much of the time, you may worry about what's going to happen to them and to you. If your parents are divorced and you live with an alcoholic parent, life can seem especially lonely and frightening. You need help coping, but you don't want to "tattle" on the parent you live with. When you visit an alcoholic or problem-drinking parent, you may fear asking for help from your other parent because he or she might cancel those visits.

Acceptance. You need to know that your parents accept you and that they still love you even when they're angry. You need your parents to notice your accomplishments and to praise you for them. You also need them to listen to your point of view, your feelings, and to care about you even though they may not agree with you.

Joyce is a sixteen-year-old high school junior who gets good grades and is on the cheerleading squad. Even though she loves school and will have no problem getting into college, that isn't good enough for her father. He wanted to be a doctor but didn't have the money for medical school, so he expects Joyce to live out his dreams. The only problem is that she doesn't like math or science, even though she gets B's in them. Joyce wants to be a social worker.

Most of the time she and her dad keep an uneasy truce, but when he's been drinking that's hard to do. "You're an airhead," he criticizes when he looks at her report card. "After all I've done for you, working a job that drives me to drink, you want to throw it all away and be an underpaid do-gooder!"

Joyce chokes back her tears at his disappointment and resolves to try harder next time. Maybe if she pleased him, *really* pleased him for once, he'd stop drinking. She thinks about taking a pre-med course in college, and the tears really start flowing. Why can't he like her for what she is instead of always picking on her for what she's not?

Joyce's father, like many alcoholics, considers his life a failure. Instead of seeking treatment for his problem and control of his life, he blames it on others and expects Joyce to fulfill his broken dreams. Since he can't accept himself, he can't begin to accept his daughter.

As alcoholism progresses or a drinking problem grows worse, people often make up complicated rules for themselves. They'll only drink at night or on weekends. They won't drink alone anymore. Instead of beer or scotch, they'll just drink white wine. It's impossible for an alcoholic to stick to such rules. Addicted drinkers feel that they're not only failures in life but at controlling their drinking, too. And they take it out on their children.

Even if Joyce gathers the courage to tell her dad how she really feels about becoming a doctor, the chances of his listening to her are small. Most alcoholics have a hard time admitting their own feelings, let alone talking about them. Listening to another person, especially when they disagree, is the last thing in the world alcoholics want. Kids with alcoholic parents hear so often that their feelings aren't okay that they hide them. Even when your world is falling apart, when you're angry or sad or scared to death, you'll tell yourself and the world that everything's just fine. Deep inside, you know it's not.

Control. Imagine playing a game in which the rules change from minute to minute. Something that's okay now might be cheating and get you kicked out of the game tomorrow. And what if you had no say about the rules or when they'd be changed? That's what living with an alcoholic or problem-drinking parent is like. The rules are constantly changing, and you have absolutely no control over them.

Sam is always in trouble at home. His mom yells at him for not doing the dishes one day and screams even louder when he does do them the next. What's he trying to do—replace her? When she's been drinking, he has to talk in a loud voice to get her attention. If he talks in a loud voice when she's hung over, he's in the doghouse. His mom turns on the TV and the stereo and leaves them going full blast when he's trying to sleep at night, but let him try something like that and he'd be grounded for the rest of his life! She criticizes him for not having friends over, and when he gets up the courage to ask a schoolmate home, she criticizes his choice in friends. It seems to Sam that no matter what he does, he just can't win.

He's absolutely right. He *can't* win. Kids and even adults need rules. Before we can do what we're supposed to, we must know just what we're supposed to be doing. Even adults are subject to laws, regulations at work, and common-sense etiquette.

Because they live in a world of highs and lows, of ups and downs, problem drinkers and alcoholics often aren't very skilled rule-makers. Whether they are angry with their kids or pleased with them has more to do with drinking than with what the children have done or failed to do. A drinking parent like Sam's mom can't be consistent or fair. Alcohol makes that impossible. The rules change, and the punishment for breaking the rules changes, too. If Sam's mother is drunk and happy, she ignores the wrong things he does. When she's drunk and angry, she overreacts, destroying his things and locking him in his room for hours. Other times she thinks the same offense—say, not doing homework—is "kind of cute and masculine," and she praises him for standing up to his teachers.

Even though you may not like to admit it to adults, you need rules so you'll know where you stand and what's expected of you. Fair and consistent rules also show you that your parents care about what happens to you. When kids are brought up with ever-changing rules or no rules at all, they feel off balance and try to force their parents into saying no and setting limits. Doing things you know are wrong can be an effective way of getting an alcoholic parent to notice you.

Other kids with alcoholic parents make complicated rules of their own and punish themselves for breaking them.

Either way, living in an alcoholic home is very confusing for most kids. You can never tell what's going to happen to you next, and you have no control over how people feel about you or act toward you.

Guidance. There's much more to being a parent than making rules and enforcing them. Parents need to be willing to listen to their kids' problems and to be ready with ideas about how to solve them. You might choose not to discuss everything with your folks, but it's nice to know you could if you wanted to. Kids, teenagers especially, may need help from their parents as they make major decisions in their lives—decisions about what career to choose, about whether or not to have sex. Parents are the ones who teach us how to act toward others; we often learn this by watching how they handle situations.

No matter how hard they try, alcohol-dependent parents are not good teachers. Debbie's mom started drinking heavily soon after she took a sales job with a real estate company. The pressure at work was just too much to bear, she said. As soon as she arrived home, she poured herself a drink, and she usually had several more before dinner. Whenever she was disappointed or nervous, Debbie's mother drank.

Debbie didn't know that stress doesn't *make* people drink, but that problem drinkers and alcoholics use stress as an *excuse* to drink. By the time she was in high school, her mom had been drinking addictively for five years, so Debbie assumed that was how everybody handled anxiety—they drank or took tranquilizers. When she failed her algebra test, she sneaked a glass of wine from the refrigerator. Before her first real date she drank half a bottle of wine to cure her nerves. The night before she had to be in a school play she drank to get to sleep. Because she'd grown up with so much drinking, it seemed natural to do it herself.

Not all children of alcoholics imitate their parents' drinking patterns, but many do. Because alcoholics and problem drinkers have trouble getting along with people, often they can't show or even teach their kids how to make up after a fight with a friend or to compromise when they disagree with a teacher. If your alcoholic parent is always fighting with your other parent, he or she certainly can't help you get along with a boy or girlfriend.

Even when a chemically dependent parent assures you that it's fine to come to him or her with your troubles, you may hold back on having heart-to-heart talks. You can't be sure how your parent will react to what you have to say. So much depends on the drinking. Some teenagers feel that their alcoholic parent has enough problems without having to share their troubles, too. When a problem-drinking or alcoholic parent does offer guidance and advice, many teenagers don't listen. How can a parent tell you how to cope with your problems when he refuses to face his own?

Independence. The older you get, the more you want to try new things and to grow up. It isn't easy learning to stand on your own feet. Neither is it easy for parents to watch their children become adults. When parents cling too tightly and treat you as if you were a little kid, they make your job of growing up much harder. On the other hand, if they push you into acting like an adult before you're ready, you don't have a chance to change and grow inside at your own pace. Because alcoholic parents are concerned totally with their own needs, they often aren't aware that you need them to let you take some risks and give you their vote of confidence when you try.

Jeff can't remember exactly when he "took over" for his alcoholic father, but it seems like forever that he's been fixing the car, mowing the lawn, and deciding which bills to pay first. Even though he holds his family together and seems very mature for his age, inside he's a scared little kid. Painfully shy with other teenagers, he avoids school activities. Instead, during what little free time he has, he paints toy soliders and reads. There's no time for dating, and even if there were Jeff would feel disloyal to his mom. There's no way he would leave her or his thirteen-year-old sister alone with his father. He's decided that after he graduates from high school he'll live at home because his family needs him. But a small voice inside tells him sometimes that he needs his family just as much, that he'd be nothing without them.

Jennifer, Jeff's sister, acts more like a fourth grader than the eighth grader she is. Her brother and mother have always treated her like a baby, pampering and protecting her. She's scared to press her clothes because she might burn herself, and she has never stayed alone in the house, not even for an hour. Jenny knows something is wrong with her dad, but she doesn't have the slightest idea what it could be. Jeff and Mom always say he has the flu, and she's never questioned that. In fact, she's never really questioned anything. It's safer not to think and not to grow up, safer to act like a little kid, drawing attention to herself and away from her father.

If you've been pushed into acting older than your age or if you've been overprotected, you know how hard it can be to fit in at school. Whether you're the family baby or the strong, dependable one, it is hard to think much about pulling away from your parents and brothers and sisters to shape a life of your own.

Faith. Usually that word makes us think of church and religion, but faith has a broader meaning. Other words for faith are belief, confidence, and trust. Even if you aren't a religious person, you still need to believe in something, you still need to trust. You need confidence, even if it's only confidence that the sun will come up tomorrow. You need a set of moral standards to tell you right from wrong. Most of us receive the gift of faith from our parents. They teach us by word and example to be kind, just, generous, trustworthy, and honest. They also help give us courage to face tomorrow.

Even though alcoholics and problem drinkers may have

started out to be upright people, the more they drink, the more wrong turns they take in life. Alcoholics don't have courage to face tomorrow or even tonight without a drink. Kindness, fairness, generosity, and trust get lost somewhere underneath the drinking. Although your parent knows right from wrong, those judgments seem unimportant next to a Tom Collins or a rum and cola. Because an alcoholic parent trusts in nothing but the next drink, it's impossible for him or her to teach you how to trust or to be trustworthy. It's no wonder that Alcoholics Anonymous calls alcoholism a spiritual as well as a physical and an emotional disease.

Betty would like to look up to her father, but she can't. He lies. In the beginning, he only told fibs, like calling in and telling his boss he didn't feel well and it must be a cold when he was really sick from drinking too much. Then he started hiding a bottle in the magazine rack beside his chair and sneaking drinks when he thought she wasn't looking. Now he can have a drink in his hand and be so drunk he's staggering and still insist he's cold sober. Last week when the police picked him up for drunk driving, he threw a tantrum and said he'd been drinking soda when his breath test proved otherwise. Betty is left with an empty ache inside. If she can't believe in her dad and trust him, whom can she trust?

Many children of alcoholics learn to trust no one. The world is an unpredictable place for them. Truth and lies are all mixed together. If parents can be so drunk they can't walk and still tell you they haven't had anything to drink, then reality must be something you invent to meet your needs. Kindness, fairness, and generosity are things you read about in books, not things you experience. And what's loyalty? It must be sticking to the same brand of beer through thick and thin.

CHAPTER IV

How Does My Parent's Problem Affect Me?

Wouldn't it be great if you could leave home to go to school or to a friend's house and close the door on your family alcohol problem? You wouldn't have to think about it or be affected by it as long as you stayed away from your house. You could take a vacation and just be yourself instead of a kid with an alcoholic parent.

It doesn't work that way. Family alcohol problems have a habit of following you wherever you go. You can walk away from your alcoholic parent, but you can't walk away from the anger, the pain, the sadness, or the worry you feel over that parent and over the changes his or her drinking have made in your life. All children of alcoholics have been shaped to some degree by their parent's drinking. Even when you grow up and leave home for good, you will still be the child of an alcoholic. You can walk away from your troubled family, but you carry confusion and emotional pain inside of you.

In the last chapter we talked about how alcoholism and problem drinking make it difficult for parents to meet their children's needs. When teenagers (whether they come from an alcoholic home or not) miss out on one or more of the essential mental health ingredients, they may have a difficult time getting along with people. They may not feel good about themselves either. How can you care about someone else when you don't feel loved? How can you take the risk of making a new friend when you feel worthless because your father is so critical of you? How can you trust other people when your mother keeps breaking her promises to you?

A Six-Pack of Negative Emotions

Children of alcoholics face several other problems besides the ones we've discussed so far. Because life with an alcoholic parent is so constantly upsetting, it's easy to become hooked on a six-pack of negative feelings: anger, helplessness, worry, shame, guilt, and sadness. There is more than enough of these feelings to go around in an alcoholic's family. Let's look at them one at a time and see how they affect you.

Anger. Many alcoholic households are filled with rage and arguing. Even when the fighting is done with words only, some kids can't do their homework or finish their meals because of the conflict. The shouting and temper tantrums may give them headaches. It's hard to sleep when people are yelling and difficult to concentrate on anything when people are always trying to get you to take sides.

Your parent who doesn't drink yells at your parent who does, to get him or her to stop. Your alcoholic parent hollers back. Sometimes both of them storm at you. All that anger is catching. Pretty soon you feel furious, too, though you may not say anything about it. You may feel angry most of the time—even when you aren't at home.

Children of alcoholics get mad at their parents for making life so difficult. It's hard to make plans and to have friends over when your parent has a drinking problem. You can't count on your parent to pick you up after the club meeting at school or even to show up sober for your graduation. When you look around and see that not all parents are like yours, you may feel cheated and betrayed. In time, you can forget just who or what you're angry at and start feeling hostile toward nearly everyone and everything. Other people say you have a chip on your shoulder—and they could be right.

Helplessness. Often alcoholic parents want their children to parent them. An alcohol-dependent mother may talk about her sexual problems with her teenage daughter and ask for advice about them. An alcoholic father may share his financial problems with his kids and ask them to suggest ways to keep the family going without money. You can't be your parent's parent. When you try, you fail and feel worse than you did to begin with. You're the one who should be getting the guidance and advice!

How much Mom or Dad drinks affects your life as much as his or hers, but you have no say in the drinking. Will you gather around the table for a big Christmas dinner or will you grab a burger at the fast-food place? Will Mom offer sympathy for the D on your report card, or will she scream at you and slap you? When your mother or father is addicted to alcohol, you have little or no say or idea about what's going to happen tonight, tomorrow, or next year. It's enough to make you feel helpless, hopeless, and out of control. You may feel like giving up.

Worry. Many kids react to an unpredictable life by worrying. Because your future is unknown, you may live in constant anxiety about what it holds for you. When your parents expect you to take care of them, you worry about who will take care of you. Certainly not your problem-drinking parent! Probably your other parent is too busy caring for the drinker to pay much attention to you.

You may worry about your alcoholic parent's health and whether he or she will get in trouble with the law or have an accident. You worry about whether the neighbors, your friends, and your teachers know about your home life. You worry that something awful may happen to your brothers and sisters. Worry can take so much time and energy that you don't have any left over for school or friendships or just growing up.

Shame. Although you love your alcoholic mother or father, it's normal if there are times when you're ashamed of him or her. People who are addicted to alcohol tend to dress sloppily when they're drunk. Their clothes may not match, their buttons don't always button, and their zippers don't zip. An alcoholic's breath usually smells bad, and many alcoholics drink to the point of vomiting or wetting themselves. Others pass out. These things may not happen all the time, but you never know when the drunkenness will happen.

Because alcohol lowers inhibitions, people who drink too much may say and do things that embarrass you in front of your friends. Your mom may start flirting with your boyfriend, or your dad may drive like a maniac when he's taking you and your friends to the basketball game. That sort of thing may not have bothered you when you were younger, but now that you are more aware of what other people think, being the child of an alcoholic can cause you shame. That embarrassment doesn't vanish when your parent isn't around or when your parent is sober.

Guilt. Even if Mom or Dad hasn't blamed you for the drinking, you still may have the idea that it's somehow all your fault. Maybe if you'd been a better kid when you were younger, or if you'd been smarter or better looking, your parents wouldn't have to resort to drinking. Maybe if you hadn't been born . . . Kids tend to blame themselves for the bad things that happen to their parents. By now you know that your parent's drinking isn't your fault, but knowing it in your head isn't the same as believing it with your heart. If you grew up certain that you caused Mom's or Dad's alcoholism, that belief has become such an important part of you that it's hard to give it up. Guilt can be a strong and crippling emotion, and it doesn't go away overnight.

Sadness. When you're old enough to understand that not all families are like yours, you may decide that you're different from other kids. You feel alone and unhappy. It's like standing outside in a blizzard and looking into a warm, cheerful room where there's a party going on—a party to which you weren't invited. You wonder how it would be to feel happy and carefree. What would life be like if your parent were like other parents and didn't drink?

Some children of alcoholics grow up feeling as though pieces of themselves were missing. They grieve for a happy childhood that wasn't possible for them.

Mixed Feelings. If we experienced only one emotion at a time, life might be easier. Most children of alcoholics feel a simmering, bubbling mixture of anger, helplessness, worry, shame, guilt, and sadness. They also love their parents and have good feelings about them.

The push-pull of mixed feelings leads to another feeling—confusion. You may hate your dad for getting drunk and hitting you, but at the same time you are sad because you want him to love you and you feel guilty for being so mad at him. Maybe you respect your Mom for taking care of everyone while Dad drinks, but you're angry with her for disciplining you and being stingy. Face it, sometimes when Dad's been drinking, he's silly and a lot of fun to be around. Mixed feelings don't mean you're crazy; everyone has them. But they do make it hard for you to think straight about what's happening at home.

"Rules" for Living with an Alcoholic Parent

All families have a set of unspoken rules—rules even more important than the don't-interrupt-the-adults and make-your-bed variety that all teenagers hear too often. One unspoken rule is that Mom and Dad are the bosses. Others might be that family members will respect each other's privacy or won't call each other names or hit each other. The rules need not be written down because everyone in the family understands them and agrees with them. The only time they're discussed is when they're broken.

Alcoholic families may seem unpredictable and disorderly on the surface, but they, too, have unspoken regulations. In fact, these family "laws" are stricter than the dos and don'ts most other families live by. Why? Because without them family members would find it very hard to tolerate living with an alcoholic and it would be more difficult for the alcoholic parent to continue to drink. Alcoholic family rules help a family to stay together and at the same time avoid admitting that there's a problem with alcohol.

These regulations make a lot of sense to and for families who struggle with alcoholism. They make almost no sense to the rest of the world. When you stick to the rules inside your family, you survive. If you try to live by those rules outside, you quickly find they don't work. Sometimes you may get in trouble because of them. You may have a hard time getting along with people, or tell untruths. Instead of talking out your problems, you may act them out. Sometimes teachers and friends think you're a little strange because of the way you act.

You're not strange; you're just doing what comes naturally for the child of an alcoholic parent. Though you may follow them automatically now, you weren't born knowing a set of alcoholic family rules. In the beginning you *learned* the rules. Now you can learn other, healthier ways to relate to people. Before you can think about choosing to use or not use the alcoholic family rules when you're outside your family, you need to know just what they are.

Rule #1: Don't trust yourself. Mixed feelings aren't the only source of confusion in alcoholic homes. The difference between right and wrong, between truth and lies, is very hard to figure out when you live with an alcoholic parent. Do you trust your ears about the argument you heard last night, or do you believe you imagined it as Mom and Dad insist you did? When you see or hear something and are told you didn't, you begin to doubt yourself. Are you losing your sight? Maybe you should have your ears checked! Could it be you're going insane?

After a while you learn to live with the confusion, the half-truths, and the lies and learn not to question them. Asking questions only makes people angry with you and eager to convince you that you're wrong. In order to adjust you have to give up trusting in yourself. You tell yourself that your thoughts and feelings are wrong, and you try not to have them anymore. Your self-confidence takes a nose dive.

Rule #2: Don't trust other people. Kids with an alcoholic parent learn very soon not to trust that parent no matter how much they love him or her. You can't count on an alcoholic. Your other parent may be so worried and upset about the alcoholism that he or she makes promises without thinking and breaks them, too. After a while you start not trusting anyone—not teachers or other adults or friends. You've discovered that you can't count on anybody except yourself.

You may know a lot of other kids your age, but you can't form deep or lasting friendships without trust. You may date, but it's difficult to feel comfortable with the opposite sex. After all, if you trust boyfriends, or girlfriends, they might eventually betray you. Some children of alcoholics distrust other people so much that they become loners. Others are convinced that no adults keep their word, and they openly defy teachers and other authority figures.

Your distrust makes sense to you and to others in your family because trusting an alcoholic parent brings nothing but hurt feelings. Not trusting is a way to protect yourself from being disappointed. Still, not being able to rely on others, not even your family, makes your life a lonely one.

Rule #3: Pretend there isn't a drinking problem. For an alcoholic to keep on drinking, he or she has to deny that alcohol is causing problems. Denial doesn't work if the alcoholic's spouse and kids don't go along with the big lie. Alcoholics and problem drinkers spend an enormous amount of time and energy trying to convince their families that they're normal drinkers. If they say, "I can quit any time," or "I don't drink any more than my friends," and it isn't true, they are trying to fool themselves and you about their dependence on alcohol.

People who are addicted to alcohol are very good at blaming everything but the booze for their problems. Soon their families become experts, too. Alcoholic families can go for years and never admit that alcohol is at the bottom of their troubles. They believe that Dad acts so weird because he's having a mid-life crisis (that has lasted for thirteen years) or that Mom is sick all the time because she has a delicate constitution.

Someone who never had an alcoholic parent might think that covering up and denying the problem is like burying your head in the sand. But when you live with an alcoholic parent, you feel you have very little choice in the matter. If a parent denies having a drinking problem, a kid can get into big trouble disagreeing. It's easier and safer to go along with the delusion that everything's fine.

Rule # 4: Don't let your feelings be hurt. Nobody wants to feel angry, helpless, worried, ashamed, guilty, and sad all of the time. If you gave in to those feelings, you'd have a hard time getting out of bed. Children and spouses of alcoholics learn soon after the heavy drinking begins that if life is to go on, they've got to ignore their feelings.

Your alcoholic parent ignores his or her negative emotions by drinking. Sometimes husbands or wives of alcohol addicts begin drinking or taking drugs in a mistaken attempt to cope with the stresses of loving someone with a drinking problem. Teenage children of alcoholics, too, may try to escape their uncomfortable feelings by drinking or taking drugs.

Whether you experiment with alcohol or drugs or try to choke back your hurt feelings without them, after a time you learn that it's best not to let yourself feel much of anything. The anger, anxiety, and all the rest are still there inside of you, but you deny them just as vigorously as your alcoholic parent denies a drinking problem.

Many kids who live with an alcoholic say they feel empty or dead inside, that they really don't care about anything. Some talk about living as if they were actors in a play. They can't afford to care, so they learn to shove their feelings so deep inside that they can go through life on automatic pilot, like a robot.

Numbing the negative emotions is a way to keep from being hurt. But it also means that children of alcoholics don't let themselves feel anything—even the positive emotions such as love. When you know you don't feel too great but aren't sure what you do feel, you are out of touch with your feelings. They haven't vanished.

Rule #5: Don't discuss the drinking problem with your family. When you deny that your parent has an alcohol problem and that it's causing problems in your life, you aren't going to talk about what's going on with your family. You're too busy trying to convince yourself that nothing out of the ordinary *is* happening. In the meantime, everyone else in your family plays by the same rules: They keep quiet, too.

Families with alcoholism don't communicate their feelings. Of course they exchange words, but more often than not those words are used to hurt, to blame, or indirectly to get what they want from other family members. It's too risky to admit feeling anything, because once they started talking, they might not be able to stop before they faced the truth about the drinking problem.

"I'd have been a traitor if I talked with my dad about what I suspected," says a woman who grew up with an alcoholic mother. "I felt very loyal to Mom and didn't want to betray her. As far as I could tell, even though she was drunk most of the time, my dad didn't know. He never said anything about it. I didn't want to break up their marriage or to cause trouble, so I kept my mouth shut."

Many children of alcoholics believe that as long as they don't talk about their negative feelings or the alcoholism, those feelings and the drinking aren't real. Keeping quiet doesn't make the drinking go away, but it does keep family members safe from hearing things they don't want to hear and it protects the alcoholic. At the same time, silence pushes family members apart so that they don't feel connected to each other.

Rule #6: Don't discuss the drinking problem with outsiders. Alcoholism is sometimes called "the family secret," and for good reason. When alcoholics and their families don't admit there's a drinking problem and won't even talk about it with each other, they're not going to discuss it with friends or strangers. Remember, they've learned not to trust.

Shame and guilt play a role in keeping lips sealed about the family secret. Many families are also afraid of what might happen if others knew about a drinking problem. Would the landlord kick you out of your apartment? Might Dad or Mom be fired? Could Social Services take you and your brothers and sisters away from your parents? (If your parent is drinking heavily, that is a possibility, but kids are rarely taken from a parent who seeks treatment and stops drinking. Sometimes fear of losing the kids will bring a parent to do something about the alcoholism.)

By keeping the alcoholism a secret, you and your family enable your parent to drink without interference. You also keep your own problems hidden from prying eyes and ears. Unfortunately, the price alcoholic families pay for silence is a high one. As long as you refuse to tell anyone what's bothering you, there's no way you can reach out for help. Without some kind of help, it's almost impossible to cope with an alcoholic parent.

Where Do I Fit In?

Even when you follow the "rules," life with an alcoholic parent can be so nerve-wracking that some kids develop physical problems. Living on a roller coaster isn't easy, especially not with a steady diet of anger, helplessness, worry, shame, guilt, and sadness. The stresses and emotional strains of having an alcoholic parent can make you ill. Stress causes headaches, stomachaches, backaches, skin rashes, and insomnia (inability to sleep). Research shows that when you're anxious or nervous you become a target for colds and flu. Feeling upset may start out being all in your head, but it doesn't stay there for long.

Psychologists who talk with children of alcoholics after they've become adults have discovered other common problems they face even when they no longer live with an alcoholic parent. Many grown-up children of alcoholics:

—have trouble telling others what they want or need;
—feel guilty because their parent drank;
—are lonely even when other people are around;
—have trouble finishing things they start;
—are too self-critical;
—cannot relax and have fun;
—become upset about changes in their lives that they can't control;
—are loyal to people who don't deserve loyalty;
—don't know how to plan for the future;
—marry an alcoholic because problem drinking seems "normal" to them.

You don't have to be the child of an alcoholic to have nervous hives or to have problems with thinking ahead. Quite a few teenagers and adults struggle with some of the troubles we've been talking about. Everybody on the face of the earth feels angry or sad or guilty once in a while.

Some children of alcoholics do manage to grow up problem-free, but living with an alcohol-dependent parent increases your chances of having bad feelings about yourself and other people. It decreases your chances of knowing how to solve your problems—the ones you face outside of math class. Your risk of unhappiness is especially high when you don't realize that alcoholism is a disease or don't understand that what goes on in your family isn't always emotionally or physically healthy.

Your parent's alcoholism affects your life. That fact can't be changed. You can change *how* it affects you by not allowing your parent's drinking to control your life. Being affected and being controlled are two different things. Thinking about your own feelings, your family's rules, and how they both shape you is an important step toward taking charge of your own life and being responsible for your own happiness.

CHAPTER V

Getting By

Kids are a lot stronger inside than most people give them credit for. When you add up all the stresses and pressures in an alcoholic home, you can see that it takes a lot of hard work just to get by. Most people don't realize how much energy and effort it takes to live out each day.

All of us cope with life's stresses in different ways. Some of us close the door, put on our headphones, and block out the world. Others jump up to clean closets or wash and wax the car when they feel "antsy." Children of alcoholics react to the family stress with their own methods, too.

Researchers have described five coping strategies that are common in alcoholic homes, ways that children of alcoholics discover to handle their confusion, conflict, loneliness, and anxiety. As you read the following sections, see if you recognize some of the things you do. It's important to remember that these coping tactics aren't used only by children of alcoholics. Everybody tries one or more of them occasionally. Kids with alcoholic parents, however, often get stuck in one or two of these rigid ways of dealing with life and cannot respond in other ways.

PERFECTIONISM
If you cope by being a perfectionist, you:

—pride yourself on being one of the most responsible people you know;

—become upset when you aren't number one or when you do less well than you wanted to do;

—are considered a leader by your friends (some people may say you're bossy);

—feel more comfortable at a club meeting than at a party;

—have a tough time relaxing; there's always so much to do!

Portrait of a Perfectionist: Craig

The oldest of four children, Craig is a model student. He's in the eleventh grade and has yet to get a grade below B. He's also on the school debating team and plays basketball. One morning a week he gets up at 4:00 a.m. to deliver a neighborhood classified-ad paper, and during the summer he earns money by mowing lawns. His clothes are always clean and neat, and his manners are impressive. Craig's classmates tease him about being an executive workaholic in training.

No one would guess that both of his parents are alcoholics. His dad, a salesman with a high-pressure job, has been getting drunk every night since Craig was three, and his mother started drinking addictively after her last child was born. Craig was in seventh grade then, and he took over changing diapers and caring for the baby weekends and after school.

Over the years his responsibilities have increased. He is the one who does the grocery shopping and laundry. He writes the notes to school when his brothers and sisters are sick. When the car breaks down, Craig is the one who fixes it. Without him, his family would fall apart.

How does he manage to stay on top of all the work he does? He keeps lists, never goofs off, and sometimes stays up late doing and redoing his homework so that it will be absolutely perfect. He doesn't have much time for friends or for dating, but he tells himself he doesn't miss a social life.

Everything goes fine for Craig until he fails to make a critical basket during a game or misses an item on a test. Then he falls apart. Lately, even when he gets 100s on his papers or is chosen to chair a committee, he criticizes himself. He ought to be doing better. Being first isn't that rewarding any more, and most nights he's too keyed up to sleep.

The responsibilities that weigh so heavily on Craig's broad shoulders include the responsibility for his parents' drinking. Maybe he should set his goals higher. He could take extra classes next year and get another part-time job. If he works harder and achieves more, his parents might stop drinking or at least cut down.

"Nothing Succeeds Like Success"

Perfectionists like Craig are superkids. Some alcoholism counselors call them family heroes or heroines. If you're a perfectionist you're calm, cool, and collected on the outside, reasonable, mature—and driven to succeed. You're also a worrier, a person who feels like a failure inside, and you have a hard time relaxing. The emotion you carry around with you most of the time is guilt for your mom's or dad's drinking problem. You probably try to make up for whatever you think you did to start your parent on the road to alcoholism. Even though people admire and envy you for your good grades, sports feats, or honors, inside you aren't very happy.

Perfectionists learn to give other people what they want. Rarely do they ask themselves what *they* want; they don't have time for that. Usually the oldest children in the family, heroes and heroines are handed the jobs their alcoholic parent can't do anymore. Often they need attention and approval. That's why they always seem to be in the spotlight.

They need structure, too. They're well organized with their lists and schedules, and they panic when surprised. While they're experts at setting short-range goals and meeting them, perfectionists have trouble planning for the long term because life with their alcoholic parent is so unpredictable.

Since superkids are so capable and independent, they may be

leaders with followers, but not many friends. Other teenagers often find them boring and too serious. When they try to loosen up and relax or lower their goals, adults may scold them for slacking off. Being a family hero or heroine is an exhausting job.

PEACEMAKING

If you've learned to cope by becoming your family peacemaker, you:

—pride yourself on being a sharing and unselfish person;

—are told often that you're a good listener or a born diplomat;

—respond to arguments by trying to get both sides to agree on a compromise;

—feel that the happiness and well-being of your family is the most important thing to you;

—understand, rather than become upset, when your drinking parent breaks promises to you.

Portrait of a Peacemaker: Beth

Nobody in Beth's family knows what they'd do without her. No matter how tough things get (and they can get pretty tough with an alcoholic dad), Beth persuades everyone to pull together. When her dad comes home from the bar where he spends most of the evening and is sick on the living room floor, Beth helps him to bed and then cleans up after him.

While her mother and her brothers and sisters are furious at her dad because he's always drunk when he's home, Beth tries to understand him. He works in a factory, and although his job pays well, he's scared of being replaced by a computer. There are five children in the family. He's got a lot to worry about, Beth thinks, and if she gets mad at him, it will only make the problem worse. She feels sorry for him and listens to his complaints by the hour.

When she's not listening to her father, she's listening to her mother and her brothers and sisters. They have a lot to be worried about as well. Her mom has a hard time making ends meet because so much of the weekly paycheck is spent in bars. She wants to go to work, but her husband is against it. Beth is trying to coax him into seeing things her mother's way. Sometimes she feels like a top-level diplomat or a psychologist.

Beth's oldest brother gets so angry at their dad that he stops speaking to him. It's Beth's job to be their go-between. No matter who has a problem or whose feelings are hurt, Beth is there to listen, to offer suggestions, and to cheer them up. When her dad forgot to stop and buy the cake for her younger sister's birthday, Beth took money she'd earned from baby-sitting and bought her a bigger cake than the one planned.

About the only selfish thing Beth has ever done in her sixteen years is to eat, and she does quite a bit of that. It's a way to soothe her own feelings, which are hurt much of the time.

"Peace at Any Price"

Peacemakers are frightened of arguments and try to avoid them at all costs. Since alcoholic households are full of conflict, anger, and problems, peacemakers like Beth have a full-time job on their hands. They're so busy taking care of other people's problems that they have little time or energy to spend on themselves.

While peacemakers are so kind and understanding that they seem to have few hassles of their own, the opposite is really true. Kids who fall into the family psychologist role are usually the most sensitive members of the family. Their feelings are easily hurt, but they bottle up their negative emotions. If a peacemaker cries, it's in the privacy of his or her own room. Because people who cope by taking care of others are so warm and caring, they appear never to get angry. They can be *very* angry, but they are experts at holding their anger inside. That unexpressed rage may explain why they become so upset when other people fight. Sometimes peacemakers try to comfort themselves emotionally by eating.

Children of alcoholics who turn to peacemaking as a way to survive within their family and to be needed tend to be nice kids. They try not to become upset, and they work hard to please others. Like Beth, they are good listeners and can put themselves into another person's shoes. Peacemakers are most comfortable when they can focus attention on others. They are "yes people," apologizing often, never disagreeing, and being careful not to impose.

Givers rather than takers, they relate to classmates and members of the opposite sex by doing nice things for them. Sometimes that means finding friends or dates for others who have problems. It can also mean feeling taken advantage of or used. If a peacemaker can't give assistance, he or she is at a loss as to how to act.

If you are a peacemaker you love your family very deeply, and you're very loyal. You spend so much time and energy trying to take care of the people you love that you can't meet your own needs. Other people seldom think to reassure you or ask about your feelings because they're sure you're doing just fine. Your biggest source of sadness is that no matter how hard you try to make your family work, it gets worse and worse as long as your alcoholic parent continues to drink.

WITHDRAWING

If you deal with family stress by withdrawing from it you:

—feel helpless to change anything most of the time;

—leave the room when your parents or other family members are arguing;

—would rather watch TV or listen to the stereo alone than go to a party;

—consider yourself a shy and quiet person;

—feel that you don't belong, no matter what group of people you're with, even your family.

Portrait of a Withdrawer: Peter

Peter is a tenth grade hermit. His room is his retreat, and he leaves it as seldom as possible. For two years he saved birthday and Christmas money so he could buy a small refrigerator to go with the TV set his grandma gave him. Occasionally he raids the family refrigerator to stock his own, but he rarely eats meals with his family.

Both Peter's alcoholic mom and his dad are a little uneasy about their son's withdrawal, but he's so quiet and causes them so few problems that they don't say anything to him. After all, he doesn't date so he's not likely to get a girl in trouble, and his teachers never even learn his name until the second semester so he's no problem in school. Besides, his younger brother and his older sister always seem to demand attention and be high-strung. Pete's parents have decided that if he doesn't bug them, they'll leave him alone.

Except for his favorite TV shows, his only interest is computers; he spends hours playing games and writing his own programs. He doesn't talk to people; he interfaces with them. When he doesn't understand his homework, he writes, "It doesn't compute," across the top of the page. Kids at school tease him about being a computer nerd, but Peter doesn't care; he wants them to leave him alone as his family does.

He can't remember back that far, but his sister says he used to be a really friendly little kid—until Mom started drinking heavily. He can recall all the loud arguments his mom and dad had nearly every night back then and hiding in his room with his head under a pillow to block them out. It seemed best for everyone if he stayed in his room more and more. The odd thing about it was that nobody seemed to notice he was gone.

"Stop the World, I Want to Get Off"

The two emotions withdrawers like Peter feel the most are insecurity and helplessness. Something's wrong in the family. They don't know what it is, and even if they did, they couldn't change it. Withdrawers react to these feelings by becoming loners.

If you're a withdrawer like Pete, chances are you have a superkid for a brother or sister. Instead of competing for attention and praise, you learned to go without by becoming something of a hermit. You don't make any demands on other people. Because you don't ask for reassurance, friendship, or praise, you don't get much if any. You may fill your time with computers or TV or reading. Some hermits listen to music or fill their lives with food to the point of overeating. When they were younger they may have had an imaginary friend or two, and they may have felt closer to their pets than to their brothers and sisters or parents.

Withdrawers' most important goal in life is to fade into the background and not be noticed. They get As in school and dress to fit in with everybody else. You can't get much more average than withdrawers. They avoid conflict and getting into trouble at all costs. Withdrawers fear anger. To make sure that people don't get angry at them, they try to make themselves invisible by adjusting to whatever happens. If Mom gets drunk an hour before their birthday dinner and calls it off, that's okay. If Dad leaves home and they see him only once a month, they adjust to that, too. Withdrawers have learned to get by without thinking, feeling, or asking questions about what's happening around them.

Underneath their calm, nothing-can-get-to-me exterior, withdrawers blame themselves for not being part of their family or accepted at school. Instead of being angry that everyone in their family ignores them, hermits feel worthless and lonely.

At first withdrawing may seem like a good way to keep out of arguments and not get their feelings hurt. The more kids like Peter avoid other people, the fewer are their chances for learning to talk with others, to listen, and to cooperate. Eventually some withdrawers escape into drugs or alcohol.

DISTRACTING

If you cope with an alcoholic parent by distracting, you:

—are considered the class clown by your friends and teachers;

—find that even your folks don't take you seriously;

—get tired of people telling you how you get on their nerves;

—are probably considered the baby of the family;

—have a hard time concentrating on anything and can't sit still.

Portrait of a Distracter: Alan

A seventh grader, Alan is driving both his parents and his teachers crazy. From the time he started kindergarten, he carved a place for himself as the "school fool." That was the year he also carved his initials into his parents' new dining room set. By the time he reached third grade, the school psychologist said he was hyperactive and gave him a drug to control his behavior. The drug helped some, but not enough to make his teachers or his family happy.

Alan prides himself on getting what he wants. If joking and playing tricks doesn't work, he'll coax, whine, and plead. The kids in his class laugh at him, not with him. Alan gets "friends" by bribing them and using blackmail. He's not above throwing tantrums or crying if those tactics get him out of trouble with the teacher or his classmates.

He can't sit still for more than two minutes, not even when he's watching TV. Instead he squirms, fidgets, interrupts, and sometimes whines. Alan talks constantly, and when people don't listen he finds another way to get their attention, usually by being clumsy.

The youngest of three children, Alan is the family baby. The fact that he's always been short for his age has meant that his brother, sister, and schoolmates often treat him like a younger child than he really is.

No one takes him seriously, and everyone in his family blames their problems on him. If he weren't such a problem, they wouldn't be spending money to take him to see a psychologist. If he hadn't been caught putting girlie pictures in his teacher's desk and making obscene phone calls to the girls in his class, his Mom wouldn't have to spend so much time in the principal's office.

Alan's constant distracting serves a useful purpose for his family. They're too busy coping with his antics to think about their real problem—his alcoholic father.

"Let a Smile Be Your Umbrella and Get a Mouthful of Rain"

Peacemakers live in terror of arguments, but distracters like Alan simply live in terror. Usually the youngest child in the family or a sickly child, a distracter is babied and protected from knowledge about his or her parent's alcoholism. His or her parents and brothers and sisters conspire to cover up the drinking. By the time the distracter is born, alcoholism has been present for quite a while. A child like Alan knows that something is wrong, terribly wrong with his family. Nobody will tell him what it is, so he responds with panic.

If you are a distracter, your family members try to keep you happy no matter how high the price. You're probably good at getting your way—so good at it that the kids at school may call you spoiled. (You'd prefer to think you're charming!) Wherever you go, you liven things up with your practical jokes and your life-of-the-party act. At home, there's usually not much to laugh about, but with you as the family comedian at least things never get dull.

All that showing off, the wriggling and the giggling, the finger-tapping and the nail-biting and the hair-twisting that irritate people so much are nervous energy bursting out. Most distracters act helpless and have an impossible time doing chores or homework. Because they're cute and convincing, they often can talk other people into doing their work for them. If distracters have a peacemaker or a hero for a brother or sister, they're all set!

Distracters make people happy; they get to be on center stage, and they get their way most of the time. Their lives sound pretty easy. They're not! Distracters walk through life afraid and unsure of just what it is they're afraid of.

REBELLING

If you've reacted to family alcohol problems by rebelling, you:

—feel your friends are much more important to you than your family;

—get in trouble quite a bit with teachers and other adults;

—drink and use drugs (Why not? Mom or Dad does!);

—are admired and envied by the kids at school for your freedom;

—have heard for as long as you can remember that you have a short temper or are a born troublemaker.

Portrait of a Rebel: Melody

Melody is in the ninth grade, and already she has run away from home three times. The last time, she had the words WILD CHILD tattooed on her arm. Her counselor at Social Services has warned that the next time she runs away she'll be sent to a group treatment home for girls. Melody doesn't care.

She'd like to get away from an alcoholic mother who verbally abuses her and a father who is too busy having affairs to even notice that he has a daughter. Things would be better at home if her brothers were closer to her, but both of them are so "good" and well behaved they make her want to throw up. Her older brother gets straight As, and her younger brother always has his nose in a comic book. There's no way she could ever want to be like them.

Her friends are a different matter. They are her real family, the people who care about her and who count in her life. She skips school and hangs out with them at the local shopping center, where they dare each other to shoplift. Usually by evening they've found someone to buy them liquor, and they end up at an older kid's apartment to get drunk.

"I hate my mother and I'm never going to be like her," Melody insists, her speech thickened by drinking. When told that she's drinking like her mother, she rationalizes, "Everybody does it."

Rarely does Melody do her homework. She can't stand her teachers and counts the days until she can quit school. School is just too hard, and you have to wait too long to get any good out of it. Sometimes she thinks she'd like to get married—she has enough boyfriends. It would really get to her mother if she got pregnant.

At the start Melody's rebellion was a way to hurt her mother and get her father's attention. Her strategy has never worked, however, because her mother is usually too drunk to know or care about her daughter's escapades and her dad is rarely at home. Now she's locked into her pattern of angry outbursts and failures.

"Born to Lose"

Family rebels are made, not born, but they often feel as if they were doomed to fail from birth. Most rebels have an older brother or sister who plays the family hero role. Since no white hats are left when rebels arrive on the family scene, they take the black ones and become the family bad guys. Any attention, even negative attention, is better than none. Other rebels turn "bad" because their alcoholic parents are especially cruel or selfish.

The emotion these kids feel the strongest is anger. Like Melody, it is often useless for a rebel to confront his or her alcoholic parent. Often the other parent won't listen, either. Furious at living in such a stressful family situation, rebels learn to keep their mouths shut about alcoholism. They may gripe about cleaning their rooms and be generally defiant, but they know better than to violate alcoholic family rules.

Rebels quickly find out that the most satisfying place to vent their anger is at school. When they are old enough to have some independence, they make friends with other rebels and stay away from home as much as possible.

If you talk back, refuse to do your school work, and don't take responsibility, you may be a rebel. Rebels often get into trouble at school and with the law. They have quick tempers and often fight other kids and even adults to add to their tough image.

Deep inside, family rebels often feel bad about themselves, even though they blame others for the trouble they get into. Their friends are just as angry and emotionally needy as they are, so they don't offer much support during the bad times.

Other kids tend to envy a rebel's rough-tough freedom. After all, rebels break all the rules. They get to goof off. They also tend to have sex at an early age and with a number of partners. Rebels have no limits, and that's what gives them problems. Some commit suicide. Others harm themselves with alcohol and drugs. They get arrested. They run away from home and are sexually abused. In reality, there's little to envy about a rebel's hard life.

Part 3

SURVIVING AND THRIVING

CHAPTER VI

Learning to Help Myself

Once you've begun to understand that your parent's alcoholism is a disease and you no longer blame yourself for the drinking, you can do better than just get by. You deserve to do more than survive; you deserve to thrive. Is that possible when one or both of your parents are drunk or hung over most of the time? Thriving with an alcoholic parent or parents isn't easy, but it is possible.

There are two ways of looking at problems that come from living with an alcoholic parent. You can see them as obstacles to happiness that you can't overcome, or you can see them as challenges. By taking the latter and more positive view, you refuse to let your life be controlled by your parent's disease.

Learning to Let Go

Alcoholics Anonymous members often recite the serenity prayer:

> God grant me the serenity
> to accept the things I cannot change,
> Courage to change the things I can,
> and wisdom to know the difference.

You already know that alcoholism is a disease and that you can't change your alcoholic parent, so it doesn't make sense to expect your parent not to drink and then to feel hurt and angry when he or she does. No matter how much you want Mom or Dad to sober up, wishing won't make it happen.

You *can* change how you react to and feel about your alcoholic mom or dad, but before you can do that you must unhook from your parent's alcohol problem. Al-Anon, the self-help organization for spouses, family members, and friends of alcoholics, calls this unhooking "detachment." In order to get free, you need to stop suffering because of the actions or reactions of your alcoholic parent. You also need to stop doing things for your parent that he or she should be doing.

Alcoholism is at the center of your life only if you put it there. Removing it to its proper place doesn't mean that you love your parent any less. Love isn't worrying yourself sick over something you can't change. Your mom or dad must make the choices. When you get caught up in worry and criticism, you don't have enough time or energy to take care of yourself.

Once you've managed to pull back from your parent's problem, you can start to find other ways to cope besides the ones you now use. Even a few small changes in the ways you relate to other people can make a big difference in how happy you feel. Sometimes you may feel so stuck in your role as a perfectionist or peacemaker at home that it seems impossible to give it up, especially when you're relating to your parents. When that happens, experiment with your brothers or sisters. Try making a change or two at school with a classmate or teacher you don't feel threatened by. Make your changes slowly, one step at a time.

Change takes practice. You need to remember that your goal isn't to become a totally new person. Your old ways of getting by have their good points. Perfectionists tend to get good grades and to be leaders; their success orientation helps them in later life. Peacemakers are sensitive to other people's feelings; that diplomacy is helpful in many situations. Withdrawers may do a lot of thinking during the time they spend on their own. Distracters are always ready with a joke. And rebels, when they use their stubborn streak constructively, get us to look at life in different ways and to find new answers for old problems.

Trying on some new ways to cope gives you choices about how you'll act in any given situation, choices you didn't have before. It's like having several outfits in your clothes closet: You can change when you're tired of looking one way; you can dress to fit the occasion. Your coping skills are very similar. The more you have, the more prepared you are for anything that comes along in life.

If you cope by perfectionism:
   —learn to relax;
   —set aside ten minutes a day just to goof off;
   —try to catch yourself when you're being bossy;
   —listen to what other people have to say instead of thinking about how you'll respond;
   —do something you aren't very skilled at and enjoy the experience without bothering about results;
   —tear up your list and see if you can survive twenty-four hours without it;
   —catch yourself when you do other people's work and delegate responsibility rather than trying to do it all.

If you cope by peacemaking:
   —try talking about *your* feelings for a change;
   —if no one will listen, start a journal or express your feelings in drawings or through music;
   —next time your schoolmates or siblings argue, try walking away instead of putting yourself in the middle (they'll survive and so will you!);
   —do something just for you;
   —learn that you don't always have to share;
   —try a new hobby that doesn't involve other people;
   —go a whole day without saying, "I'm sorry";
   —make a list of all the things you've wanted to do but were afraid to try and *do* one of them!

If you cope by withdrawing:
 —write down one task you want to finish today and do it;
 —if you don't think you can finish, ask someone for help;
 —start a conversation with another person, even if it's about what show to watch on TV;
 —make note of the choices you exercise every day, from deciding what to wear in the morning to deciding what to eat for a midnight snack;
 —if you're a hermit, start taking field trips away from your "cave";
 —ask somebody to watch TV, play a computer game, or listen to music with you.

If you cope by distracting:
 —spend some quiet time alone reading a book or playing records, even if it's only for five minutes at first;
 —when you feel a joke or some silliness rising to the surface, stop yourself and ask, "Is this really funny?";
 —volunteer for a project at school;
 —start helping around the house;
 —find something to do that is relaxing to you;
 —if you start feeling panicky and hyper, take a few deep breaths and tell yourself, "Easy does it!";
 —secretly do something nice for another person.

If you cope by rebelling:
 —learn to talk it out rather than act it out even if you have to talk to yourself to begin with;
 —find new and more positive ways to express your anger. If you're not ready to talk about it, try poetry, artwork, or acting;
 —experiment with asking for what you want;
 —let somebody do something nice for you;

—try taking on some responsibility at home or at school and showing others and yourself that you can handle it;

—if you make a mistake, learn to admit it; lightning won't strike you if you say you're sorry.

Change takes time. Often it's difficult to relax when you've been tense for years (relaxing makes you nervous!). It can be hard to act responsible when you feel like a helpless little baby inside. Change is worth the effort it takes. When we change our behavior our inner feelings often change to match our actions. When you whistle in the dark and pretend you aren't afraid, even when you're cringing inside, your fear dissolves.

One way to encourage yourself to change when the world doesn't seem either to notice or to care is by using affirmations, positive statements about the kind of person you want to become. These private pep talks really work! If you're used to withdrawing and want to make a friend or two, some sample affirmations might be:

"I'm a very likable person."
"I act friendly toward others."
"Other people want to be my friend."

Affirmations are most powerful when you write them down and read them to yourself several times a day. They are a way to pat yourself on the back when no one else will, and they're a powerful antidote for the "Yes, buts" and the "I can'ts."

Make a list of the things you'd like to change about yourself. Now pick one or two items from the list and try writing some affirmations for them. Try reading them aloud to yourself when you wake up and before you go to bed at night. If you feel depressed take a few minutes and read your affirmations.

Close your eyes and picture yourself as the kind of person you want to be. If you're shy, you might see yourself talking to a good friend. If you want to be more calm around your problem-drinking or alcoholic parent, picture that. Creative daydreaming isn't always a waste of time; sometimes it can boost your courage.

Easy Does It

It is important as you try to change things about yourself to understand that you won't change overnight. Some days you'll find detachment very difficult. You'll wind up fighting with your alcoholic parent and then withdrawing or rebelling. Or maybe, even though you're trying as hard as you can to stop it, you'll throw yourself back into being the class clown with a passion. Everybody makes mistakes. Unless you're superhuman, you will, too.

You'll make your life a lot easier if you work on one thing at a time. Your major goal is learning to thrive despite your alcoholic or problem-drinking parent, but break that into smaller subgoals. One of these might be to stop taking over your parent's jobs, such as showing up at parent-teacher conferences for your younger brothers and sisters. Then work on that goal *just for today*.

Why just for today? Why not for tomorrow and next week and next month? Because the tasks ahead of you can be overwhelming. When it really starts to sink in that no matter what you do or don't do your alcoholic parent may keep right on drinking, that can be depressing. The days of struggle stretch endlessly ahead of you. How much easier it is to promise yourself that you'll cope for today, that you'll get through the next twenty-four hours. That's a goal you can reach. When you set your goals for weeks and months and years ahead, it's too tempting to give up. Many small successes are better for you than one huge failure.

One way to keep your emotional balance and feel better about yourself is to do something nice for yourself every single day. You know from living with an alcoholic parent that you can't count on something nice happening to or for you if you just sit around waiting for it to fall from the sky. Your life is far too unpredictable for that.

You know, as well, that alcoholic parents are often selfish. They're so wrapped up in their drinking that they don't have the time or the energy to meet anyone's needs but their own. Your other parent may have the same problem, except that instead of being hooked on booze, he or she is hooked on the drinking problem. If your needs are to be met, you will need to meet them. You can do that by deciding on one thing you'd like to do today for you and then doing it. Some choices might be:

—taking half an hour to read a book that isn't required reading for school;

—going for a walk and enjoying the scenery;

—calling a new friend.

Make a list of nice things you could do for you, presents you could give yourself. As you think of them, add more things to your list. Now do some of them!

Sticky Situations

Life is full of choices, even though sometimes it doesn't seem that way to children of alcoholics. Often it seems that no matter what they try to do they end up hurt or sad or angry.

When Barb's dad is supposed to drive her to a club meeting she can't miss and he's so drunk that he weaves back and forth across the road, it doesn't seem that she has any choice but to go with him and be scared, since her mother can't drive. She's glad he didn't take the car and drive away to some bar, but she feels trapped anyway. She does have choices. Learning to thrive in an alcoholic home is a matter of discovering your options and then choosing the right one or ones for you.

When a sticky situation like Barb's comes up, you might want to discuss it with your nondrinking parent. Being careful not to place any blame, ask for suggestions about what you might be able to do. Even if your nondrinking parent doesn't want to talk, you can still do some problem-solving on your own. The first step is to brainstorm. Take a few minutes either alone or with your nonalcoholic parent and write down all the ideas you have for coping with the problem. Don't stop yourself from writing as many as you can, no matter how stupid or silly some of them sound. The idea is to get as many solutions down on paper as you can.

When Barb and her mother finished her list, it looked like this:

1. I could baby-sit and do housework while Mom takes a driver's ed class.
2. I can pay attention to how much Dad is drinking so I'll have time to call someone else for a ride. Possible people:
    Jill's parents
    Grandma and Grandpa
    taxi
3. I can talk with Dad when he's sober and tell him how much his drunk driving scares me. Maybe we can make an agreement that if he's been drinking and I need to go somewhere, he'll give me taxi fare.
4. I can stay home.
5. I could just go ahead and ride with Dad if the club meeting was an important one.
6. I could lock Dad in his room without anything to drink before it was time for him to take me.
7. I could walk to the meeting, and if it's dark by the time it ends maybe someone would give me a ride home.

8. We could move to town so I'd be closer to school.
9. I could spend the day and night with Aunt Kathy, who lives close to the school.

When she had finished her list, Barb already felt less trapped. Now it was time to decide what would work. Obviously, suggestions six and eight weren't realistic; and even though Barb's mom agreed to think about number one, it would take some time to manage. Barb's club meetings were important to her; she hated to miss them. Getting out and talking with other kids was one of the things that helped her stay happy even though she lived with an alcoholic parent. But riding with her drunken father was so terrifying that she felt too sick at her stomach to have fun when she got where she was going.

Barb finally decided that she would try to talk with her father about her fears when he was sober. Her mom agreed to help her. If Dad didn't agree to pay her taxi fare, Barb could quietly call someone else to pick her up and take her to the meeting. The next best solution would be to spend the day and night at her aunt's house.

What are your sticky situations? Many children of alcoholics have a hard time doing well in school because their parent is drunk at night and there's too much noise. Other kids with alcoholic mothers or fathers want to make friends and invite them home, but they're embarrassed to have them meet their drunken parent. Still others are puzzled by what they ought to tell their friends about their parent. Your problem might be a mother who drinks and smokes: You're afraid she'll start a fire. One solution might be to buy a smoke alarm and install it in the house. That's taking control rather then being controlled. It's also getting a good night's sleep.

Write down the problem times when you feel as though your parent is completely controlling your life. Now brainstorm some solutions. Discuss them with your nonalcoholic parent or with your brothers or sisters. If you feel comfortable doing it, talk with your alcoholic or problem-drinking parent, when he or she is sober, about what would be the best solution for you.

Even though you can't know ahead what your alcoholic or problem-drinking parent will do (he or she doesn't know either), you can plan your own life. To thrive in an alcoholic family, you'll need to make several plans of action so that you have something to fall back on if your first choice fails. That way you'll gain some control over your life instead of being totally controlled by your alcoholic parent and his or her alcoholism.

In addition to discovering ways to live your own life, you need to find ways to cope with the stresses that come from living with an alcoholic parent. Kids with alcoholic and problem-drinking parents usually hit on several ways to handle stress. Not all of their tactics are good. Some overeat or drink. Others are hyper and have annoying nervous habits like chewing on their hair or biting their fingernails. Some kids try to battle stress by taking drugs. None of these ways work. Most of the time they end up creating more stress than you felt to begin with.

You already know that ranting and raving does you little good, and neither does worrying or getting depressed and staring out the window for hours at a time. Ignoring how you feel and trying to swallow your negative emotions can be even more harmful, because they tend to build up and then explode when you least expect it.

Fortunately, there are several very effective tactics that you can use to calm yourself when your home life gets to be too much.

Guided imagery. Psychologists say that it's impossible to feel two opposite emotions at once. (When you have mixed feelings, you bounce back and forth between two feelings like a tennis ball.) One way of dealing with stress and bad feelings is to squeeze them out by filling your mind with pleasant thoughts. If Mom or Dad gets you down, imagine you're walking through woods or visualize the ocean pounding on a sandy beach. If you can teach yourself to do that rather than brood, you'll cool down and feel better much faster.

Remember a time when you felt very calm. Imagine where you were. What did you see? What sounds surrounded you? Did you smell pleasant aromas? What did you feel against your skin or beneath your feet? Could you taste anything? If you have trouble recalling a relaxing time, imagine you're in the mountains or at a lake. Choose an imaginary place where you would like to be. Breathe slowly and deeply as you think of how all of your senses respond to that place. You might want to write down your fantasy field trip to read to yourself when you are anxious, or maybe even tape your descriptions and play them back.

Controlled relaxation. Lie down and close your eyes. Tighten your leg muscles as much as you can and then relax them; feel the tension flow from them. That tingly heaviness you feel in your legs is relaxation. One by one tighten and release the different parts of your body, your hands and arms, your shoulders, your stomach, your neck, your face. When you've finished, lie still for a while and breathe slowly and evenly while you enjoy the way your body feels.

Physical exercise. This can be both calming and mood boosting. Instead of climbing the walls, run around the block or do some exercises to music. Somehow expending energy physically gives you more physical and emotional energy to cope with your problems. You'll feel better, too. Many kids with an alcoholic parent have become so caught up in their parent's problem that they've forgotten to take care of their bodies. Often they feel tension in the form of aches, cramps, and stiff, sore muscles. If you're one of them, you might try getting involved in a sport that lets you get rid of negative energy and have fun at the same time. Volleyball, throwing a Frisbee, softball, and karate are some ideas. What physical activities appeal to you?

Taking a vacation. Sure, you'd love to go to Europe for a month or maybe the Caribbean for a couple of weeks. For most kids, that isn't possible. You *can* take a mini vacation, though, even if it's just to the local shopping mall or a jog around the block. Leaving the scene of your stress can give you the perspective you need right now. Even if you can't physically get away from it all, you can escape for a while into a book, a movie, or a TV show. Withdrawing all the time isn't a good idea, but taking short breaks from your troubles helps you to solve them in the long run.

Thinking positively. This is probably the hardest thing to do, but its effects are very powerful. If you can think of some of the good things that the stress of living with an alcoholic parent is doing for you, you stand a chance of transforming the stress into a plus in your life. What can possibly be good about having an alcoholic parent?

Living with an alcoholic parent may have caused you to be more independent than you'd otherwise be. Maybe your parent's alcoholism has taught you up close how disturbing an addiction can be. Perhaps you feel closer to your brothers and sisters than you would if your family didn't have the problem it does. It may take time to think of anything positive. Making the best of a bad situation is never easy, but it's a step toward making that bad situation better.

CHAPTER VII

Reaching Out for Help

Whether they need to talk with someone about their parent's drinking problem or want to find out how to do the latest math assignment, children of alcoholics have an unusually hard time asking for help. When people offer them friendship or assistance without being asked, children of alcoholics tend to turn them down. That's unfortunate, because relationships with people outside of your immediate family can make life a lot easier for you.

If you were to write down all the people and organizations you could turn to when you needed help, how many would you have on your list? Many or a few? The further an alcoholic parent progresses into his or her disease, the more isolated that person's family becomes. Family members of alcoholics cut themselves off from the outside world out of shame and fear of giving away the family secret. The more they pull back into themselves, the easier it is for the alcoholic to control them and manipulate their feelings.

Many teenagers who live with an alcoholic parent are so distrustful and so used to being completely independent that they don't recognize help when it's offered. Tiffany refused to attend the alcohol rap group being organized by one of her school counselors. She was sure that the group would be boring and that she knew more than the rest of the kids attending. Even though sometimes her loneliness felt like a physical ache inside of her, she was sure she didn't need "sitting around complaining with a bunch of dumb kids." Besides, she didn't want their pity.

Other teens are so unsure of themselves that they want to be rescued or saved and make unwise choices about who helps them. When sixteen-year-old Will started dating Jessica, she was like the answer to his prayers. She listened to him and cared about him, which was more than his problem-drinking parents had ever done. At fifteen, she was more like a mother to him than his own mother. He had been tempted to marry her before she became pregnant, but now that she was going to have his baby he felt trapped and betrayed, and he started to drink heavily himself. The answer to his problems turned into an even bigger problem than he started with. No way could Jessica save him from his parents!

Maybe you're a bit skeptical about what a solid network of friendships and other sources of emotional support can do for you. If so, take a look at the facts. Researchers have found that:

—people who can confide in others and share their emotional burdens have fewer health problems than those who don't;

—self-help group members are better adjusted and happier than people with the same problems who avoid such groups;

—adults who use more "we's" than "I's" have fewer heart problems than those who are self-centered;

—people with a number of close friendships tend to live longer than loners.

Reaching out for help may not be easy to do right now, but it's worth the effort. Anything that can help you to feel happier and healthier and to live longer is worth a little work.

One of the best places to begin is to open yourself to the possibility of forming friendships with kids and with other adults who aren't part of your immediate family. Even when you don't discuss the problems you face living with an alcoholic parent, these friendships can help you cope at home. In the first place, they help you to feel better about yourself. Friendships with other kids can give you a better perspective on your home life and a chance to see how other families operate.

Making friends with adults, whether they're neighbors, aunts and uncles, teachers, or youth leaders, gives you an opportunity to learn to trust others. Knowing that some grown-ups keep their promises to you is an important lesson. Some researchers who have studied children of alcoholics believe that outside relationships keep you from being emotionally damaged by your parent's alcoholism.

Although relationships with kids your own age and with adults are very important, sometimes they aren't enough. When you need more than friendship, try talking with a school counselor or making contact with an alcohol treatment program to find out if you can get counseling there. Ministers, priests, and rabbis are often willing to talk with you. If they don't know much about family alcoholism, they can probably put you in touch with someone who does.

At the end of this book are listed several organizations of interest to children of alcoholics. You might want to write to them and see what help they can offer you.

Make yourself aware of other books about alcohol and alcoholism besides this one. Although there aren't a lot of books written specifically for teens, you can learn a good deal from material aimed at adults. The more you learn about alcoholism and living with an alcoholic parent, the easier it will be for you to talk about your problems. (A book or pamphlet may be a good starting point for a talk with your nonalcoholic parent.)

Many children of alcoholics find special help in groups of teens who share their problems and concerns. It's easier to open up and talk about what's worrying you with kids who know what it is like to live with an alcoholic mother or father. These groups are often connected with alcohol treatment programs, or they may be offered through your school. They're called rap groups, peer counseling groups, mutual support groups, or self-help groups.

As teachers, counselors, and mental health professionals become more aware of the special issues you face because of a family alcohol problem, they are starting rap groups all across the country. If you can't find one near you, you might talk with a school counselor or someone who works with an alcohol treatment center about starting a group.

Rap groups and peer counseling can be very effective because everyone knows what everyone else is talking about. You don't need to go into lengthy explanations. When you join a group you can learn how other kids cope and find out that you aren't alone. After listening for a while, you'll find that your experiences and ideas can be helpful to some of the other kids in the group. Being able to help other people helps you to feel better about yourself. To find out about these groups, ask your school counselor, local alcohol treatment center, and the local chapter of the National Council on Alcoholism. You might also write to Community Intervention, an organization that works with schools to set up rap groups.

Alateen

The largest and best-known self-help group for children of alcoholics is Alateen. A division of Al-Anon, a fellowship for family members and friends of alcoholics, Alateen was started in 1957 by a seventeen-year-old boy whose father was a member of Alcoholics Anonymous and whose mother belonged to Al-Anon.

Alateen meetings are free and welcome any teenager who has an alcoholic parent. (If you're a preteen there are meetings for your age group, too.) Unlike a "club," Alateen membership is constantly changing. When you go to a meeting, you won't be the new kid for long. Neither do you have to worry about somebody at the meeting telling outsiders that you were there. Kids in Alateen don't reveal each other's names, and since only first names are used during meetings, you can keep your privacy.

Speakers and discussions are focused around the Twelve Steps, which are borrowed from Alcoholics Anonymous. Alateen members follow the program, progressing through the steps at their own pace, but with help and encouragement from other members.

ALATEEN'S TWELVE STEPS

1. *"We admitted we were powerless over alcohol—that our lives had become unmanageable."** You can't control your parent's alcoholism or your alcoholic parent. A mother or father with alcoholism affects your life and makes it difficult. Their alcoholism isn't your problem to work through, but you can solve *your* problems, the ones that come from living with an alcoholic parent.

2. *"[We] came to believe that a Power greater than ourselves could restore us to sanity."** Whether you believe in God or not, Alateen members feel that believing in something outside of and more powerful than yourself will help you. Another way of putting this is "letting go and letting God."

3. *"[We] made a decision to turn our will and our lives over to the care of God as we understood Him."** Before your Higher Power can help you, you need to decide that you want help.

4. *"[We] made a searching and fearless moral inventory of ourselves."** Instead of focusing on your alcoholic parent's flaws, you need to take a long, hard look at yourself. Along with your shortcomings, you must discover your strengths and good qualities. This step helps you to know yourself.

5. *"[We] admitted to God, to ourselves and to another*

---

*"Twelve Steps and Twelve Traditions for Alateen," published by Al-Anon Family Group Headquarters, Inc.

human being the exact nature of our wrongs.'' It's important to share your insights about yourself with others. That means overcoming pride, and it isn't easy to do. It is necessary to do to develop honesty, straight thinking, and humility.

6. *"[We] were entirely ready to have God remove all these defects of character.''* Some of your bad habits may be old friends. You may be using them as an excuse or as a crutch, and it can be frightening to get rid of them. Alateen members suggest substituting the opposite good habit for a bad one.

7. *"[We] humbly asked Him to remove our short-comings.''* This step means admitting that you can't change yourself completely on your own. You need a focus outside of yourself to help you.

8. *"[We] made a list of all persons we had harmed and became willing to make amends to them all.''* It is much easier to make a list of all the people who have hurt you than of all the people you have harmed. When you focus on your past mistakes and drop the old excuses, you learn not to take your feelings out on other people.

9. *"[We] made direct amends to such people wherever possible, except when to do that would injure them or others.''* You need courage to practice this step. Even though you can't undo the past, you can take responsibility for your mistakes and lessen their damage. You have nothing to lose but your guilt.

10. *"[We] continued to take personal inventory and when we were wrong, promptly admitted it.''* Being aware of your actions and correcting them when they need correcting is a never-ending process. Another word for that process is growth.

11. *"[We] sought through prayer and meditation to improve our conscious contact with God as we understood Him, praying only for knowledge of His will for us, and the power*

to carry that out.''* You need to find quiet time to communicate with your Higher Power in order to gain serenity and a sense of purpose in life.

12. *"Having had a spiritual awakening as the result of these Steps, we tried to carry this message to others and to practice these principles in all our affairs."** It isn't enough to get help for yourself and stop there. You must help others in the same predicament. By practicing Alateen principles in other areas of your life, you can turn your pain at being the child of an alcoholic into real gain.

If you would like to attend an Alateen meeting, you can learn about times and locations by calling the number listed under "Al-Anon" in your phone directory. When Al-Anon isn't listed, you may be able to get the information from Alcoholics Anonymous. If you live in a small town or a rural area, write to Al-Anon Family Service Group headquarters. If they can't find a group near you, they can help you start your own. All it takes are two people!

You Don't Deserve Abuse

Teenagers can be abused by parents just as younger kids can. Just because you won't be living at home much longer, or because you're not a cute little kid anymore, doesn't mean that abuse isn't serious. Child abuse is never okay, and there isn't a child or teenager who deserves to be abused. Abused teenagers need help.

Although not all alcoholic parents are abusive, kids from alcoholic homes have a greater chance of being abused than do other children or teenagers. This abuse takes three forms: physical (hitting, slapping, punching), sexual (remarks, touching, and actual intercourse), and emotional (belittling, verbal cruelty). Let's take a closer look at these three types of abuse.

—Most of the time Josh gets along pretty well with his alcoholic father; the two of them share many interests such as camping, baseball, and woodcarving. But ever since Josh can remember there have been times when Dad would get irritable, then drink and fly into uncontrollable rages. The first time he hit his son was when Josh at thirteen tried to stop him from punching his wife in the stomach. Josh's mom was pregnant at the time. His dad turned his anger from her to his son, punching him in the mouth and loosening two teeth.

The next day Dad came home with flowers for Mom and an expensive model Josh had been wanting for months. He acted sorry and was the perfect father—until the next time he got angry and drunk. That night he burned Josh's mother with cigarettes and beat Josh with the cord to the electric frying pan. Now, two years later, there's a pattern to the abuse. The tension starts to build, and it peaks when Dad, a binge drinker, goes out and gets drunk, then comes home and beats his wife and child. Afterwards he makes up to them, and both Josh and his mom hope things will be okay, but they aren't. The tension always builds, and the beatings that follow get worse and worse. Josh is scared of his dad, but he loves him, too. He's afraid to tell anyone about the beatings for fear something awful will happen to his father, so he suffers in silence.

—Luanne's trouble began when she was ten and her mother started working nights because her problem-drinking father had lost his job. The first night Daddy came into her room and collapsed on her bed, Luanne wasn't scared. She was more disgusted. Here he was drunk again, and even if he wasn't yelling, he was ruining her sleep when she had a report to give tomorrow. Dad's nighttime visits persisted. Before long he was crawling beneath the covers and hugging her and touching her in ways that felt bad to her.

She shuddered and shrank away from him, but he wouldn't stop. He wanted her to touch him, and then he forced her to have sex with him. Luanne felt dirty and used, but because her father threatened to say she was lying if she told their "secret," she kept it to herself. Once she did try to talk about it with her mother, but before she was able to confess what had been going on for four years, she figured that Mom wouldn't believe her. If anyone would be punished and taken away from the house, it would be she, not her father.

—Vickie's problem isn't as obvious as Josh's or Luanne's. Vickie suffers from emotional abuse. Both her alcoholic mother and her dad who doesn't drink at all constantly tease and belittle her. Even though he's never so much as spanked her, her dad has threatened to shoot and stab her. He's never needed to spank any of his kids, he tells anyone who will listen. He has them trained. He doesn't tell his children that he loves them; instead he repeatedly tells Vickie that she's no good.

In all of her sixteen years, Vickie can't remember her mom ever smiling at her or holding her. Her mother has repeatedly told her that she was a "mistake" and shouldn't have been born. Even though her mother has a college degree and years ago worked as a teacher, Vickie has suffered from neglect at her hands. When Dad worked at a sales job that took him out of town for days at a time, Mom often forgot to feed the children. Often they went to school unwashed and in dirty clothes. Even now, if Vickie didn't clean the house or cook the meals, it wouldn't be done.

If you recognize yourself in the stories of Josh, Luanne, or Vickie, you are probably a victim of abuse. It can be frightening just to admit it, to acknowledge what you've suspected all along—that not everybody's parents punch them or slap them or push them down the stairs. Not everybody's parents act in sexual ways toward their children. Not everybody's parents reject their kids or neglect them or batter them with cruel words. What is happening to you isn't right.

It isn't always the alcoholic parent who beats, molests, or emotionally abuses his or her children. Sometimes the parent who doesn't have a drinking problem may grow so bitter, angry, and anxious that he or she is the abuser. A father may inappropriately turn to his daughter for comfort and sex when his wife has a drinking problem. A mother may scream at her young children and try to control them with physical force because she feels that her life with an alcoholic husband is completely out of control.

If you feel that the parent who isn't abusing you will listen to you and can offer help, talk with that parent. Sometimes a quiet talk will give you the understanding you need and persuade your parent to seek help for you and your family. Other times it just makes him or her angry so that both of your parents seem to be your enemies. Then on your own you'll need to find help outside of your family.

Why is it so hard to get outside help when you're hurting so much? For most children of alcoholics, keeping a family secret is second nature. They've practiced denial and are very good at it.

Just as important, even when you have been physically, sexually, or verbally abused, you probably still care about your parent. If you "tell," what will happen? Will Mom or Dad be punished? . . . or get help? . . . or hate you?

If you wait for your alcoholic parent to see the light and stop abusing you, you may wait forever. If you protect your parent at your own expense, he or she won't get better. The same holds true when the abusive parent doesn't have a drinking problem or alcoholism. Getting help may be the hardest thing you've ever done, but it's the smartest, too. Sometimes taking your problem outside the family is the thing that motivates your parent to recognize his or her alcoholism and do something about it.

You can start by talking with a teacher you trust, your school counselor, or your doctor. By law they are required to report suspected cases of physical and sexual abuse to the proper authorities. It is more difficult to get help for emotional abuse, but you can ask for their suggestions.

Most communities have a child-abuse "hot line." The telephone operator will know the number and give it to you. Child welfare and child protective services departments of city and county government are also good places to seek help. For more information about physical, sexual, and emotional abuse, you can contact:

The National Committee for Prevention of Child Abuse
332 South Michigan Avenue
Suite 1250
Chicago, IL 60604

Part 4

WHAT NEXT?

CHAPTER VIII

What About My Parent?

If you've been trying some of the suggestions made in the last two chapters, probably you are starting to feel somewhat better about yourself and more in control of your life. Chances are that you're having some big doubts, too. The choices you're making may seem quite selfish to you. They don't deal at all with how to get your parent to stop drinking. Even though you know now that there's no way you can force your parent to admit the problem and do something about it, you still may be wondering if there's anything you can do to help.

When you think about all the awful things that happen to alcoholics who continue to drink, the detachment or letting go we talked about earlier may come hard for you. You need to know that unhooking from your parent's alcoholism is the best thing you can do for him or her right now. When you remove alcohol and drinking from the center of your life and act as though it has no power over you except the power you give it, you demonstrate to your parent that alcohol isn't the most important thing in the world. That's a strong message, stronger than lectures or nagging or arguments.

Unhooking from Your Parent's Alcoholism

Only about one alcoholic in every thirty-seven admits having the disease, gets treatment, and stops drinking. Because you love your parent, you want him or her to be one of the lucky ones. Alcoholics' chances of recovery are much greater when they have a job and a family, two things they stand to lose if they keep on drinking. Their chances of recovery increase even more when their family doesn't cover up the disease or make it easier for them to drink. Before alcoholics are willing to seek treatment, they need to carry the burden of the disease alone and feel its staggering weight. Helping your parent carry the burden means that your parent will be able to drink longer and will get sicker.

The more family members protect and "baby" an alcoholic, the fewer reasons that the alcoholic has to stop drinking. Covering up for an alcoholic or a problem drinker may seem like a "nice" thing to do. It isn't. When Dad gets drunk and loses his car keys, and you find them for him, not only do you enable him to drive drunk, but you show him that he's not responsible for taking care of his belongings. When Mom's cigarette burns a hole in the carpet because she's passed out, and you just make sure there's no fire and don't bother her with it, you protect her from her alcohol-induced carelessness. When you smooth over the little problems in an alcoholic's life, you're getting rid of your parent's warning signs that there's a bigger, and maybe even a life-threatening, crisis coming in the future. Those warnings are points of choice for an alcoholic. Take them away and you ensure that your parent will keep on drinking.

Wouldn't just telling your alcoholic parent to stop drinking work just as well? Even though you say you do it for the alcoholic's "own good," arguing, nagging, blaming, and try- ing to make your alcoholic parent feel guilty do no good. Often they serve as ways to vent your anger, to relieve your bad feel- ings for a minute or two, but they don't help Mom or Dad come to terms with the disease. In fact, they can hide what's really wrong (the addictive drinking) behind a screen of name- calling, angry words, and hurt feelings. More often than not, Mom or Dad will use your outrage as yet another excuse to drink.

The strategies kids and nonalcoholic parents use to get a family member to stop drinking often backfire. You start out wanting to save your alcoholic parent, but somewhere along the way you get attached to the disease again and become as unhappy and twisted in your thinking as the alcoholic is. Before long you're feeling worse than you did before, and your alcoholic parent is drinking just as much as before, if not more. You're in a frustrating and vicious cycle.

Often children of alcoholics want their parents to stop drinking so badly that they decide they'll *force* them to quit. The first tactic that usually comes to mind is to pour the booze down the sink. Even though it seems like a great idea, the first tactic is also the *worst* tactic!

For years Randall had known something was wrong with his dad. All through elementary school he hadn't been able to figure out what was the matter. His mom always said that Dad was a highly emotional person when he asked her about the temper tantrums and the depressions. Randall's older sister said that their father was a free spirit who just didn't fit into a conformist world. The neighborhood kids hinted that his father might be a mental case. Seeing the unsteady way his father walked, sometimes Randall was afraid that Dad might have a terminal illness.

By seventh grade Dad was still around and none of the explanations quite fit the case, so Randall was still looking for answers. That year his science teacher showed a film about family alcoholism. During the entire movie Randall sat in the darkened classroom with a dry mouth and a stomach so heavy that it felt as if it were full of rocks. His dad was an alcoholic! His slurred speech and mood swings were from drinking. At first Randall felt stupid for not catching on; then he was gripped by a sense of betrayal and anger.

By the time he got home, Randall was a man with a plan. While his parents were both at work, he found his father's store of scotch and poured it all down the toilet. His heart pounding, he waited for his father to return. He waited quite a while, because his father often had to "work late." (Randall now suspected he was having a few after-work drinks.)

"You're an alkie!" The words burst from a tightly packed

place inside of Randall the minute Dad opened the front door. He felt better the instant they were out.

He didn't feel better for long.

"Marge," Randall's father called to his wife, "it's enough I have to listen to *your* whining. Now you've got the boy started, too!" He moved to the liquor cabinet and discovered it was empty. "Who did this?" He roared like a bull.

Suddenly Randall's plan didn't seem as smart as it had that afternoon. "I did," he managed to squeak. "And if you buy more, I'll pour that out, too."

"Not if you want to leave your room again before your fortieth birthday!" With that, Randall's dad left for the liquor store. He didn't come back that night or the next. When he finally did return, it was with two black eyes, a case of scotch, and a sturdy lock for the liquor cabinet. Randall's pouring the liquor down the john hadn't done a bit of good. In fact, it had done the opposite.

Getting rid of an alcoholic's liquor is more upsetting to you than it is to the alcoholic. Think about it for a minute. Booze is everywhere. All your parent needs to do is go to the liquor store, the grocery store, or a bar and he or she can drink again. When you get rid of the liquor in the house, the only thing you're doing is provoking your parent. Alcohol is readily available, but you can't find a replacement parent quite so easily. You're faced with a furious parent who's still drinking.

Kids who try to get rid of the booze often do so because they feel helpless and angry. Often they aren't quite sure at whom or what they ought to be mad. Alcohol can be a tempting target. When you want to pour Mom's or Dad's liquor down the drain, remember that it won't cause them to stop drinking. Alcoholism, not alcohol, is the cause of your parent's problems. There's absolutely no way to pour your parent's alcoholism down the drain!

Another mistake many children of alcoholics make is to argue with their parents. Dawn, a tenth grader, tried using logic and her skills as a junior member of the school debating team to persuade her mother and father to give up drinking. She even practiced her speeches in front of the mirror in her room. After weeks of arguing herself hoarse, she gave up and felt like a failure. Her parents still drank. The only thing that had changed was that now they thought she was a smart-mouthed teenager.

Most people, even when they don't want to hear the truth, will eventually listen to reason. Not alcoholics! Alcoholics don't listen straight because they don't think straight. Argue with people who have had too much to drink, and they'll ignore you or think you said something you didn't. Then they'll begin to argue back, and they won't make any sense, but you can't tell them that. Because people who are drunk have lowered inhibitions, they may be quicker to yell or scream or even lash out and hit their opponents—even when those opponents are their children. At best, you'll walk away from the big argument with a headache and your stomach tied in knots. Your alcoholic parent can just have another drink and block it all out.

The denial that is so much a part of alcoholism is a powerful tool that alcoholics use to make the people around them doubt what they see with their own eyes and hear with their own ears. When Annette's mom came home drunk and parked the car right in the middle of the lawn, running over her daughter's 10-speed bike, Annette blew up at her. After her mother finished with her, Annette wasn't sure what had happened. Her mom made it sound as if Annette had run over the car with her bike! She was still angry, but now she was puzzled, too. Was she at fault for leaving her bike in the yard? Was her Mom really drunk, or *did* she have flu? Alcoholics are experts at deflecting blame from themselves and tossing it right back to the person who has confronted them.

Should you argue with your parent between spells of

drunkenness? Even though your chances of being mistreated either with words or slaps is lower when your parent isn't drunk, arguing with an alcoholic isn't worth the energy it takes. Mom or Dad may feel guilty and apologize, promising never to drink again. The chances of that really happening are almost nil unless he or she admits being an alcoholic and gets some form of treatment. That is a choice your parent must make when she or he is ready. With professional help, your family may be able to speed that decision, but you can't argue it into happening.

It isn't unusual for a temporarily sober alcoholic or problem-drinking parent to grab a beer, a glass of wine, or a shot of something in response to what you've said. Then he or she can turn to you with the ultimate put-down: "How can you say you want me to quit drinking when you're driving me to drink?" Alcoholics excuse their drinking by telling themselves that nobody understands them. Your arguing proves that. Self-pity has so clouded their thinking and feelings that alcoholic parents can't see things from your point of view. You can't win an argument with an alcoholic or problem-drinking parent—not about drinking. It's far better to use your energy and your time to make your own life better. If your parent starts the argument, calmly walk from the room or listen without responding. Verbally defending yourself won't get you anywhere if your parent's been drinking.

Some kids think that if they make Mom or Dad feel guilty enough, their parent will give up drinking. Even though they may not act like it, alcoholic parents already feel more guilty than you can probably imagine. Your mother or father probably uses that guilt as yet another excuse to drink. Alcoholics have a disease. They need treatment, not guilt trips. Sometimes when you're feeling bad and need some attention, it may be tempting to play "poor me" in front of your parent. When that happens, think about how you'd act if your mom or dad had heart disease or diabetes instead of alcoholism.

Trying to tell your mother or father how to get and stay sober isn't a wise idea either. Once you start acting like a therapist or a parent to your mom or dad, you get caught up in the disease again. Your lectures, nagging, and helpful hints, even though well intended, serve no purpose but to make you responsible for the drinking. That responsibility belongs to your parent, not to you.

Many alcoholics do reach a point when they know deep inside that they've crossed the line between psychological and physical dependence, though they wouldn't admit it to another person or even to their own conscious mind. They make rules for themselves to regulate their drinking. If your parent is in the middle stages of alcoholism, you've probably heard these statements many times before: "Well, at least I don't drink before noon." "I'm never going to drink alone again." "I like beer too much, so I think I'll switch to vodka and orange juice for a while." It is a rare alcoholic who can keep the rules. As long as the alcoholism progresses untreated, the person who has it will get sicker and sicker.

You can, if your parent expresses in interest in treatment, tell Mom or Dad about A.A. or treatment centers you've heard about. It's also fine to give encouragement and moral support. It can feel very good to be helpful and to feel needed, but remember you *aren't* an alcoholism counselor and your parent isn't your client.

Finally, stop yourself from making threats. They have little or no effect on alcoholics despite the fact that they are very much afraid of losing their children's love or their children. If you've ever yelled, "I hate you and if you don't stop drinking, I'm running away!" then you know that is true. Your mom or dad probably went right on drinking. When you make threats you can't or won't carry out or that are harmful to you (like running away or getting drunk), you're just giving Mom or Dad "more trouble" and another excuse to drink. If you really do feel like harming yourself, you need help from a counselor, social worker, psychologist, or minister—not your alcoholic parent.

It is impossible to teach an alcoholic a lesson by threats. Alcoholics understand that threats are powerless because they themselves make them all the time right along with the promises they make and break. Then too, there are usually so many harsh words and so much anger bouncing around an alcoholic household that nobody notices one more outburst.

You've already started figuring out the choices you have in sticky situations. Use those choices to solve your problems, not to threaten or bully your alcoholic parent. If your father is drunk and too noisy while you're studying for a test, think of your options, then pick the best one and do it. If it means going over to a friend's house to spend the night—fine. Calmly tell your parent where you're going in as few words as possible, then go.

Now you know the things *not* to do when you have an alcoholic parent:

—Don't pour the liquor down the sink. Getting rid of the drug doesn't get rid of the disease.

—Don't argue with your parent about drinking. You can't win an argument with a drinking alcoholic.

—Don't try to make your parent feel guilty about drinking. Would you do the same to an undiagnosed diabetic?

—Don't try to tell your parent how to get sober. Leave that to the professionals.

—Don't make threats.

Actions Speak Louder Than Words

What *can* you do to help? If you're making some changes in how you think about your parent's drinking and react to it, you're already having a profound effect on Mom or Dad, even though it may not appear so on the surface. You're showing that it is possible to live life without being controlled by alcohol, alcoholism, or an alcoholic even if you live with that alcoholic. Learning to take care of yourself has other benefits for your parent, as well.

According to Toby Rice Drews, an alcoholism counselor and author of *Getting Them Sober,* alcoholics have an 80 percent better chance of getting sober when their families use tough love. What is tough love? It's letting your alcoholic parent hurt enough to want to get well.

To keep drinking and never question their addiction, alcoholics have to convince themselves and you that you desperately need them, and couldn't live without them. You may know (and they probably know deep inside) that the reverse is true. When you stop arguing and begging and become quietly independent, you take both the alcoholic and his or her disease out of the center of your life. When the world no longer revolves around your parent, he or she may begin to have second thoughts about the drinking. If you don't depend on him or her, maybe you eventually won't put up with the drinking and drunken behavior. That thought can be very scary to an alcoholic.

Just refusing to take the blame any longer for making Mom or Dad drink means you'll walk a little taller and with a firmer step. You'll smile more, and you won't let your home life get to you quite so much. This change in attitude, too, can be very unsettling to an alcoholic parent. If no one in the family takes the blame for making Mom or Dad drink, and if no one takes responsibility for Mom's or Dad's actions when drinking, he or she will start to sag beneath the weight of the alcoholism. The sooner alcoholics start thinking about their drinking, the sooner they can face the facts and get help. When you don't prop up your parents, but give them the responsibility and dignity of solving their own problems, you raise the chances of having that happen.

If you really want to help your parent get better, you'll need to stop lying and start telling the truth. That means no more covering up. Certainly, you aren't going to stand on a street corner and announce, "My parent is an alcoholic." That wouldn't do any good. What does work is to stop pretending your parent is acting normally and to avoid situations in which you have to make up an excuse or a lie about your parent's behavior. Take yourself out of the middle between your alcoholic parent and the consequences of his or her drinking.

Alcoholism counselors use the term *enabling* for the game-playing and fibbing that go on in alcoholic families, because they enable or help the alcoholic to continue drinking without having to think that he or she might have an alcohol problem. Are you an enabler? Some things an enabler might do are:

—going to school for parent-teacher conferences for younger brothers and sisters when a parent is drunk and saying the parent is sick;

—making excuses to the neighbors the morning after a party for a drunken parent's insults or loud music;

—telling an alcoholic parent that everything's fine when it most definitely isn't;

—driving an alcoholic or problem-drinking parent to the liquor store when he or she is unable to drive.

Let's say Mom asks you to call her boss and say she's so sick she can't come to the phone, let alone work. What will happen if you do it? She'll be able to drink to the point where she's unable to go to work and not have to take any responsibility for it. If you don't lie, she'll have to solve the problem by herself. At first she may try to solve it by yelling at you or drinking more heavily, but neither of those strategies will work. Eventually, she'll be faced with coming to terms with her alcoholism problem or losing her job.

Ed was excited by his big role in the school play. For weeks he'd been learning his lines and rehearsing. On opening night he wanted nothing more than to have Dad reasonably sober and sitting in the audience. But that morning his father started drinking, and Ed was afraid that his father would be too smashed even to drive him to school. His mother said that maybe she could get Dad to drink enough coffee that afternoon to sober him up, but Ed knew it wouldn't work. It hadn't before.

He called a friend and arranged for a ride to school. Then he thought about the play for the balance of the day instead of lecturing, nagging, or threatening his father, who continued to drink. When it was time to leave, Dad was very drunk. Taking a few deep breaths, Ed quietly and firmly told his dad that he was going to the play with a friend and that he hoped Dad would be able to attend the next evening. He asked his mother to go with him, but she said she'd feel too guilty leaving her husband, so Ed went alone. It was a difficult decision, but one he could feel good about afterward.

Often you'll start out practicing tough love alone, especially if your other parent is still hooked into the spouse's alcoholism like Ed's mother. Stand your ground and know that even though it isn't always easy, it is the only way to make your life and your family life healthier and to help your alcoholic or problem-drinking parent.

Family therapists tell us that when one family member changes, eventually other family members change. These changes happen slowly, not overnight. If you start going to Alateen meetings, maybe your brothers and sisters may start attending. When your other parent sees that you seem calmer and happier, he or she might want to try an Al-Anon meeting. Be careful not to play the boss or know-it-all. People hate to be pressured into doing things—even things that are good for them. If you go about getting help for yourself without trying to push or force your parents or your brothers and sisters to follow suit, you may be surprised at the positive changes you'll start seeing in your family.

What happens when you forget and make a mistake in the way you handle your parent? You forgive yourself and begin again. Nobody's perfect. If you find yourself arguing, nagging, lecturing, or begging your alcoholic parent to stop drinking, chances are that you have some very strong feelings about what's going on. Don't bottle them up. Instead find a way to communicate those feelings to your parent, a way that won't backfire. The answer for you may be gentle but firm confrontation.

Pick a time when Mom or Dad hasn't been drinking to open the discussion (not an argument). Make sure you "own" your own feelings rather than trying to blame your parent for causing them. You'll want to stick to specifics, too. If you can bring up an incident that happened recently, it will have far more impact than talking about "drinking too much." Alcoholics really can't believe, until they've undergone treatment and stopped drinking, that it's ever possible to drink too much. A calm, "I was worried and scared when I was riding with you yesterday and you got the traffic ticket for driving under the influence," does far more good than, "You made me so upset that I broke out in hives yesterday because you were drunk again." Saying, "I love you and I wish you'd stop drinking," has more weight than blaming or angry words.

Once you understand the disease of alcoholism and can unhook from your parent's alcohol problem, once you're getting help for yourself, you may want to carry your confrontation a step further and participate in what alcohol professionals call an "intervention." In an intervention, an alcoholic's family members, close friends, and sometimes even employers form a confrontation team led by a trained alcoholism counselor. One by one team members calmly confront the alcoholic with the facts. They try to make the truth come between the alcoholic and his or her disease. As the evidence about his or her drinking piles up, the alcoholic's denial system starts breaking down. When an alcoholic can no longer deny having a drinking problem, it is very difficult to resist treatment. Usually the alcoholism counselor and the husband or wife of the alcoholic have chosen a treatment center before staging the intervention, and the alcoholic signs in that day before he or she can strengthen the denial defenses again.

Interventions offer new hope to alcoholics and their families. As you talk with others in Alateen or with an alcoholism counselor, you may learn more about them. You might want to share that information and hope with your nonalcoholic parent. A word of caution, however: You cannot stage a one-person intervention, and it is very risky for a family to try to organize one without a professional leader. Misusing a powerful tool like intervention can be more harmful than helpful.

CHAPTER IX

When a Parent Recovers

Suppose it really does happen. Your mother or your father recognizes the problem, decides not to drink anymore, and takes steps to get help. What happens then?

Obviously, when your parent stops drinking you will experience major changes in your life. Some of them will be improvements but, surprisingly, you may not like some changes at all. While your parent is trying to give up alcohol, you will need to adjust to a new way of family life. Even when that new way is better than the old, it will take some getting used to. Old habits are hard to break.

All change is stressful, even the happy changes. Suppose you'd been wanting to date somebody at your school all year long. Then all of a sudden that person asked you out or you got up the courage to ask. The night of the date, you'd be happy, but you'd be nervous, too. When a parent stops drinking, it can be like that. You've wanted the drinking to stop for so long. Now that it's happened, you may feel anxious and have a hard time believing your parent's recovery is real. Living with a parent who is recovering from alcoholism means big changes for everyone in the family. Your parent's treatment may require that he or she spend days or weeks in a hospital. For the first three days your parent is "detoxing," metabolizing all the alcohol from the system. Detoxing from alcohol isn't pleasant. Some people say it feels worse than physically unhooking from heroin. If a person was an extremely heavy drinker, the process can be physically more dangerous than detoxing from heroin. That's why many alcoholics stop drinking in the hospital. It is safer for them to be watched by doctors, nurses, or medical technicians than to try sobriety alone.

Next Mom or Dad will start seeing an alcoholism counselor in the hospital, go to group counseling meetings with other patients, probably attend Alcoholics Anonymous meetings. Those meetings help him or her to learn how important it is to stay sober and how to cope with problems in other ways besides drinking.

After a time, your parent's counselor may want to talk with you, first alone and then with all the members of your family. Some teenagers are frightened by that because they aren't sure what role they're supposed to play in their parent's recovery. Many treatment centers believe that family therapy helps the recovering alcoholic, his or her spouse, and their children adjust to life without alcohol. Just as recovery is a healing time for your mother or father, it's a time for healing your hurt feelings and bad memories, too. Only when your parent has "graduated" from the hospital alcohol treatment program will he or she be allowed to come home.

Even if your parent kicks the alcohol habit at home, Mom or Dad will probably be attending counseling sessions or A.A. meetings. Often newly sober parents need to attend such meetings every single evening in the beginning. You may feel as abandoned and left out as you would if your parent had gone away for treatment.

Those feelings are normal, but they can be especially strong if you thought your life would change for the better the minute Mom or Dad decided not to drink. Maybe you want to start doing things as a family again and make up for all the times you missed while your parent was drinking, but all your parent does is read booklets about alcoholism, stare out the window, and go to A.A. meetings. Doesn't your parent love you? What's wrong?

Nothing! Starting an alcohol-free life is very difficult. Your parent's first priority is to get and stay sober. Only then can

Mom or Dad turn attention to improving his or her relationship with you. If your parent tries to do too much at once, there is a high risk of going back to the bottle. By going to meetings and putting every ounce of energy into staying sober, your parent *is* giving you a loving gift, even though it may not seem so at the time.

Those first few days and weeks aren't going to be easy for anybody. If your parent goes to a hospital or drug treatment center, you may be frightened of the unknown changes that are taking place in Mom or Dad. If your parent begins recovery at home or comes home from in-patient treatment, you may still feel as if your life is out of control. The experts believe that it takes at least a year before all of the family pieces fall into place.

"I wanted it so much to happen and I wanted it to be happening right now," says Lucy, an eighth grader. "I guess I believed that some doctor was waving a magic wand over my dad at the hospital. You know, that he'd come home a different person. Well, he was the same in some ways, but in other ways, I thought he was worse. Don't get me wrong, I didn't want him to keep drinking. I just didn't know he'd be a grouch when he stopped."

Often recovering parents *are* grouchy in addition to being very concerned with their sobriety. Lucy's dad had given up his security blanket, his beer, and he didn't know quite how to act anymore. Remember that alcohol is an anesthetic and a depressant. When alcoholics drink, they don't notice much about their surroundings. Their senses are dulled, and they focus almost entirely on one drink and then the next. Living without alcohol is not easy in the beginning. Every sound, including your stereo, seems louder to your parent. Every light seems brighter and more irritating. We talked earlier about how addiction to alcohol means that an alcoholic feels best with alcohol in the system. Without it the cells rebel. It takes time before your parent feels good again.

Besides being grouchy and short-tempered, many alcoholics become deeply depressed when they stop drinking. Some researchers say that this overwhelming sadness has a physical cause, but others have a different explanation. Old habits, even the most destructive ones, become like old friends. Some alcoholics think of their drinking as being as much a part of them as an arm or a leg. They need to go through a grieving period when they give that habit up because it's like losing a friend or a very important part of themselves.

Sometimes your parent will have a strong craving for a drink and will need to turn all of his or her attention to not drinking. At other times Mom or Dad may feel cheated and deprived because other people can drink, but they can't. Often recovering alcoholics are very frightened about whether they can cope. When adults are scared, they tend to hide it behind anger.

More than likely, you've wanted your parent to stop drinking for a long time. Now that your wish has come true, you're a little scared about the unknown changes ahead, but you're happy, too. You want to do everything you can to help Mom or Dad stay sober. Like many other teens of recovering alcoholic parents, you'll try to be very careful what you say and do. If you aren't prepared for your parent's moods, you may believe that Mom's or Dad's irritation, depression, or preoccupation with meetings is your fault. Something you've done is making them reject you or feel unhappy. That's not true. It is a way of thinking you started when your parent was drinking addictively, a way of thinking you need to work to correct now.

What Do You Expect?

You need to know that some parents stop drinking only to start again. Alcoholism counselors call that a relapse. Many recovering alcoholics relapse several times before they finally stop drinking for good. Those relapses, if they happen to your parent, aren't easy for you to cope with. You have high hopes and then, overnight, those hopes are dashed and you feel as if your parent and your family were back at square one. That isn't so. Even if recovering alcoholics take a step backward for every two steps forward, they're making progress. It's your job to make sure you don't blame yourself for your parent's relapse.

"I was really shocked when I came home from school and Mom was drunk again," says Max, who is sixteen. "She'd been seeing a therapist and going to A.A. meetings sometimes twice a day. She seemed so excited about having another chance. Then she messed it up. I was so disappointed and so mad at her I wanted to shake her."

Max expected that his mother would never take a drink again, and he hadn't even heard about relapses. When he saw his mother had been drinking, he felt betrayed and angry. Anger is a common reaction when our expectations aren't met. Most often they aren't met because they're too high. It may be impossible for a recovering parent to meet them.

If you start feeling angry or bitter, you might ask yourself whether you want too much too soon. Sometimes kids of recovering alcoholic parents hope for many unrealistic changes. If your parents argued often and talked about getting a divorce, you may want them to get along now. They might do that, but more likely they will still argue as they work through their problems. Eventually they'll argue less, but not now. Another possibility could be that they'll go ahead and get a divorce.

Maybe your dad grumbles about money problems. You may think that if he stops drinking he'll be able to get a better job and then you'll have all the cassette tapes and clothes you want. You'll have a car and a big allowance and . . . Hold it! Just because alcoholics stop drinking, that doesn't mean they'll be rich or famous or even happy.

So why stop drinking? Because when alcoholics recognize their addiction, they take control over their lives. They can make decisions and have choices. Their chances of leading a happy and fulfilled life increase dramatically, and so do chances for their family life to improve.

When a parent stops drinking, it doesn't guarantee a good marriage, lots of money, or happiness. It does offer a chance for a better life. But you shouldn't expect miracles from your parent's sobriety, even though it is a trap many teens fall into.

When a parent becomes sober you *can* expect that:

—life will become more predictable; you'll have some idea of what's going to happen next;
—it will eventually be easier for you to talk with your parent and feel you're being heard;
—you will be able to trust your parent in time.

It is unreasonable to expect that:
—you'll always get your way;
—you and your parent will always agree and never argue;
—you will immediately develop a close and trusting relationship with your parent.

Talk It Out, Don't Act It Out

—Stephanie was excited and hopeful the day her mom poured the last of the white wine down the sink and promised never to drink again. Ever since her dad had moved out five years ago, Stephanie had felt that her mother ignored her. Between work and dating and drinking, it didn't seem to Stephanie that her mother even knew she had a daughter.

A month after her mom stopped drinking, Stephanie wasn't so sure she liked living with a sober mother. Sure, now Mom cooked the meals and they were on time and she stayed home many evenings, but Steph felt trapped. All of a sudden Mom wanted to know who she was going out with and when she'd be home. Mom had a serious talk with her about her bad grades and insisted that she pick up her room, things her mother hadn't noticed or cared about when she was drinking.

Stephanie found herself picking arguments with her mom and calling her names. She "accidentally" left magazines open to wine ads on the sofa and her mother's favorite chair. "You don't have any right to tell me what to do, you old alkie," she told her mother, and then she began staying all night at friends' houses. She had mixed feelings about her mother's sobriety, and she was acting them out rather than talking them out.

—Arnold had always felt overworked when his dad drank. Since he was the oldest child, he watched his brothers and sisters after school and did many of the household chores. In addition, he mowed the lawn and took over some of his father's tasks like maintaining the car and making home repairs. He thought he'd be happy when his father came home from the treatment center. He was for a while, but before long he missed being the man of the house. It felt as if no one in the family needed or wanted him around anymore. Because his feelings of rejection were so strong, he wanted to block them out, so he started drinking with a gang of kids from school. A month later, he ran away from home and was picked up by the police.

When an alcohol-dependent parent stops drinking, the family has new rules and new roles. Mixed feelings like Arnold's and Stephanie's aren't unusual. Naturally, a lot of bad things were happening when your parent drank too much, but probably there were some benefits for you as well. If you could ask Dad for your allowance, then ask him again when he was drunk and had forgotten he'd paid you, you aren't going to feel too happy going without double allowances. If Mom never cared where you were going or about your grades, you aren't going to feel overjoyed when she stops drinking and notices your flaws.

Many teens, like Stephanie and Arnold, have a hard time putting their negative feelings into words. It can be both frightening and painful to admit those feelings to yourself, let alone your parent. If there's a secret part of you that wishes Mom or Dad still drank, are you a terrible person? No way! Mixed feelings happen to the best of us.

We get in trouble when we choose not to talk about those negative emotions. They bubble and boil inside of us until they have to get out somehow. Stephanie provoked arguments, disobeyed her mother, and called her names. Arnold went from being the best kid on the block to the worst. Other teenagers in their position might hit their brothers and sisters or stop doing their homework so they'll fail in school. Some teens eat everything in sight, and others stop eating. There are lots of ways to act out, but none of them can help you solve your problems the way talking can.

During your parent's recovery it is important both for you and for your parent to communicate. Walking on eggs and trying not to upset each other may work for awhile, but not for long. Remember that you and your parent would disagree sometimes even if Mom or Dad hadn't experienced a drinking problem and recovered. All families have some conflicts.

It would be easier for you if you could rely on your parents to start talking, but that's not always the way it works. People who drink addictively or who live with addictive drinkers often do everything they can to avoid being honest with other people. They hide their feelings. Your recovering parent and your other parent may find it difficult and frightening to start talking with you and listening to what you have to say. Mom or Dad may feel very guilty about past behavior and be terrified that you'll say you hate them.

Sometimes it's up to you to make the first move. Communicating isn't easy when you're not used to it, but with practice you can learn to share your feelings—even the negative ones—without starting World War III. Some good ways to share your feelings without getting into big arguments are:

—Try to solve problems rather than win arguments. Be willing to compromise. Too often, the only way to "win" arguments is by hurting other people and damaging relationships.

—Be careful not to blame other people for the way you feel. The quickest way to make parents stop listening is to say, "It's all your fault!"

—Stick to what you really want to talk about. If you're sharing how you felt when Mom or Dad was drinking, then talk about the past. Otherwise don't drag up past hurts. If you say, "You never loved me when you were drinking" during an argument about your allowance, that's not fair.

—Own your feelings instead of pushing them off on other people. Say, "I am angry when I think you're treating me like a baby," not, "You treat me like a baby and make me angry."

—Learn to listen. If you want your parent to listen to you, it's a good idea to return the courtesy.

—Avoid absolutes. Words like "always" and "never" trigger arguments. Use more accurate words like "sometimes" and "not often."

—Know when to quit. Sometimes you or your parent may be too upset to think or talk straight. If you're going around and around without solving your problems, agree to take a break and discuss things later.

No matter how hard you try, you may not be able to share your feelings with your recovering parent or your other parent. When that happens, it's still important to be able to talk with someone about what's going on during your parent's recovery. You might share your hopes and fears, your dreams and hurts with your parent's alcoholism counselor or a teacher or counselor at your school. Maybe there's a friend from Alateen who would listen to you and give you moral support. Remember that talking it out is better than acting it out, even if talking is sometimes a more difficult thing to do.

Rules of the Road to Recovery

By this time you're probably suspecting that your parent isn't the only person in your family who is going through recovery. You are, too, and so are your other parent and your brothers and sisters. Your whole family is taking a walk down the road to recovery. Here are some things to remember so you won't get lost along the way.

1. Recovery takes work. The passage of time alone doesn't make your hurt feelings or your insecurities disappear. Time, by itself, isn't going to get your parents and you talking again. It is true that recovery takes time—many months—to get rolling, but without work, time doesn't really help you feel better or your family get along better.

2. When a parent stops drinking, that doesn't solve all of a family's problems. It gives a family a chance to solve its problems. The troubles that were caused by your parent's drinking will ease up when your parent quits. But some problems were there before the drinking, and others that started because of the drinking have grown until they have a life of their own. Stopping drinking is the beginning of recovery, not the end.

3. Your parent will never be able to "make it up to you" for his or her drinking. The past is the past, and there's no way to go back and undo it. After you've looked at your feelings and shared them, you need to unhook from them. You can't change the past, but you *can* make the most of this new beginning.

4. If your parent starts to drink again, remember that the relapse isn't your fault. You didn't make your parent drink, and you can't make him or her stay sober. Whether your parent's recovery succeeds or fails is not on your shoulders.

5. Live one day at a time. It took a while for your mom's or dad's drinking to develop into alcoholism. Then it took much longer for your parent to admit to a problem and to stop drinking. Recovery doesn't happen overnight.

CHAPTER X

Will I Become an Alcoholic?

In Chapter II we talked about how common the disease alcoholism is, striking one out of every ten drinkers. We said, too, that a predisposition toward alcoholism is probably inherited, just as hair and eye color are handed genetically from generation to generation. Does that mean you'll be an alcoholic like Mom or Dad?

No, but it does mean that your risk of alcoholism and drinking problems is higher than that of other teens whose parents aren't alcoholic. Here are the facts we know now:

—Half of all alcoholics have alcoholic parents.

—If you include brothers and sisters, grandparents, uncles, and cousins, about 95 percent of all alcoholics have an alcoholic relative.

—Children with an alcoholic biological parent (as distinguished from a stepparent) have a four to five times greater risk of becoming alcoholic than other kids.

—About a third of children with alcoholic parents grow up to be alcoholics.

—Some, but not all, types of alcoholism seem to be sex-linked, passed from mother to daughter and father to son.

It would be the same if one of your parents had diabetes or high blood pressure. Since you know that these health problems tend to run in families, you'd watch your salt or sugar intake carefully. You'd become aware of the physical signs of diabetes or have your blood pressure checked occasionally so that if you had inherited either of those problems, you could seek early treatment. Children of alcoholics need to understand that their chances of developing a drinking problem or physical addiction are greater than those of most people; they need to make themselves aware of the warning signs.

But I'm Never Going to Drink!

Some kids with alcoholic parents don't take even a sip of beer, wine, or liquor because of their bad memories about alcohol. Even if they have an inherited predisposition to alcoholism, they aren't going to take a gamble and learn about it the hard way. These abstainers, however, are a small minority.

Even though they never touch a drop, they still may face alcoholism problems—problems that come with an alcoholic spouse. According to a recent study, if you are raised in an alcoholic home you have one chance in four of growing up to marry an alcoholic. The reasons are simple. Children of alcoholics have learned to tolerate behavior that other people consider abnormal or bizarre; they have memorized how to live with an alcoholic. Remember those family rules and the ways kids cope? Often it's easier to keep in the same old rut and find an alcoholic to spend your life with than it is to change.

Although you may vow to yourself that you'll never drink or be at all like your alcoholic parent, things can happen to change your mind. Most kids with alcoholic parents eventually do drink, even if only socially. After all, two out of every three people in the U.S. drink alcohol. Nobody wants to feel like an oddball! Teenagers especially may feel enormous pressure to drink:

—Ninety-three percent of high school seniors have tried alcohol.

—Seventy percent use it once a month.

—One out of every five high school seniors drinks daily.

—Some researchers think that as many as one third of teenagers can be classified as problem drinkers.

—Studies indicate that teenagers are doing more binge drinking (getting drunk) than before.

—Kids in their teens often take drugs and alcohol in combination. Sometimes those drug/alcohol mixtures can be killers.

If you've chosen not to drink and you can stick to your resolution, more power to you. If you drink even though you've promised yourself you wouldn't, you aren't alone. Children of alcoholics may feel the impact of peer pressure even more than other kids because they feel like loners, different from the rest of the kids. They may not be used to having close friends and may feel awkward or uncomfortable with kids who aren't from alcoholic homes and who live by different rules. For some of these teenagers, alcohol can be a way to belong, a way to fit in.

Unfortunately, several factors besides heredity and peer pressure push children of alcoholics toward problem drinking, whether they begin as teenagers or as adults. Children of alcoholics are at risk for other drug dependencies, too, whether illegal drugs or prescription drugs such as tranquilizers. First there are the coping roles that children of alcoholics learn to play at home. Let's take one last look at them.

Perfectionism is a no-win struggle. No matter how hard you try, you can't be perfect. If you set unrealistic goals and fail to meet them, you'll feel rushed, pressured, and disappointed a good deal of the time. Perfectionists don't usually drink heavily in school or college. It's later on that the tension they live with catches up with them. Then they may drink to unwind after a tough day and to tranquilize themselves to sleep at night.

Since *peacemakers* carry on their shoulders the burdens of

those around them, they subject themselves to a good deal more stress than humans were intended to handle. If you're a peacemaker, you may be drawn to drinking to calm yourself. More than likely, though, you'll be tempted to use alcohol to help keep your anger inside and ease the pain of never having your own needs met. The high price of peace is often the peacemaker's own peace of mind; many try to regain it with alcohol.

Withdrawers want to avoid the world. Drinking and taking drugs are very effective ways to do that. Alcohol is a way to distance yourself from the people around you. It's also an anesthetic, a way to blot out not only the world, but one's inner feelings.

Kids who *distract* and who exist to be the life of the party often feel that they need to drink. Drinking makes them feel more in control and that their inner panic doesn't show. Because our society thinks of liquor, wine, and beer as icebreakers and social lubricants, distracters may consider them important pieces of equipment. Because alcohol lowers inhibitions, they may think they give their best performances drunk. Some distracters are hyper; for them drinking may be a way to slow down.

If you're into *rebelling,* you know that social drinking is important if you want to be accepted by kids in your circle. *Anti*-social drinking may be just as important. Rebels want to be rough and tough, so they hang out with tough kids. Tough kids are usually heavy drinkers and drug takers. For a rebel, drinking is part of a carefully constructed image. Heavy-drinking teens frighten and anger adults. They break the rules of how kids are supposed to behave, and that's what rebelling is all about.

One of the characteristics of a problem drinker, according to the U.S. Department of Health and Human Services, is drinking in an attempt to cope with life. Perfectionists, peacemakers, withdrawers, distracters, and rebels all can easily add alcohol to their coping patterns. It gives them the illusion of handling life's stresses and problems, temporarily dulls their emotional pain, and gives them enough false confidence to scrape through the day.

Children of alcoholics must deal with other pressures. All through childhood and adolescence we check out what the important adults in our lives do, and we copy them. Sometimes we do this without even being aware of it. Parents may say, "Do as I say, not as I do," but kids rarely listen. Instead they imitate.

If you've lived with a problem-drinking or alcoholic parent, you've learned some important lessons, even if they were bad ones. You've learned that the thing to do when you're feeling nervous or out of sorts is to drink. You've learned that adults "solve" their problems by drinking. Needing a drink to get through the day isn't odd to you; after years of living with an alcoholic parent, it can seem perfectly normal—just like passing out at night and throwing up in the morning.

Even when say we're never going to be like our parents, most of us copy the way we've seen our parents behave. If we don't know that we need to watch out for being "like father like son" or "a chip off the old block," we may not know why we behave the way we do. Once we understand that sometimes we imitate our parents without thinking, we have a choice about how we will act. We can choose to behave like our parents or we can choose to behave differently.

How Do I Know When I'm in Trouble?

Most heavy teenage drinking is irresponsible drinking, not alcoholism. Even so, the idea that you can't have a serious drinking problem until you are an adult is false. You need to realize that there are teenage alcoholics and that if you have a genetic predisposition toward alcoholism, you might be one of them.

You know you have a drinking problem if the following descriptions fit you:

—You spend most of your time partying or thinking about partying.

—Your grades start to suffer because drinking is getting in the way of studying.

—You drop old friends who don't drink much if at all for new ones who drink as much as you do.

—It becomes harder and harder to get up in the morning. Some mornings you're late to school; some mornings you stay home sick.

—You sneak alcohol from your parents' liquor cabinet. You might even pour water into the bottles so they won't notice any is missing.

—You've lied if your parents have confronted you about your drinking.

—Your parents try to hide your drinking from school officials and neighbors or make excuses for you.

—You feel as if your life is on an emotional roller coaster.

—You drive drunk.

—You've injured yourself or another person because of your drinking.

—You do things when you're drunk that you wouldn't do sober.

—You're afraid that your drinking is out of control.

If you recognize yourself in *any* of these statements, you need to talk to a professional alcoholism counselor. Together you can figure out just how big your problem is. On your own it's very hard to determine if you're psychologically dependent on alcohol or physically addicted. In either case the counselor will have suggestions about what you can do. Your options run from an adolescent inpatient treatment program to individual counseling and teenage Alcoholics Anonymous meetings.

No matter what kind of help you choose, it can be difficult to kick a heavy drinking habit while you live with an alcoholic parent. Sometimes your concern about your own drinking can be very threatening to your parent: If you have a drinking problem, maybe he or she has one. That's a possibility few problem drinkers want to face. Sometimes, however, parents decide to get help for their alcoholism when their children seek alcoholism counseling.

Problem-drinking and alcoholic parents can make it rough for you to stop or decrease your drinking and get the emotional support for your decision from outsiders. Because you are a minor, some alcoholism counselors may be afraid your parents will cause them trouble if they counsel you against their wishes. But a growing number of teachers, school counselors, and alcoholism professionals believe in offering help despite the risks, so hang in there and keep trying—you'll find the help you need.

CHAPTER XI

Happily Ever After?

Sometimes the problems of growing up in a home where a parent is an alcoholic can seem overwhelming, especially when you think about your own future. Can you grow up to live happily ever after? Even though being happy all the time is unrealistic, and it's true that you can't undo your past, you can learn from it and heal from it. That's exactly what thousands of adult children of alcoholics are doing today in hundreds of self-help groups across the country.

More and more children of alcoholics are openly and honestly sharing information about the challenges they faced growing up and the challenges they face long after they move away from home. Each new story that is told and each new voice added to the movement bring new insights into the issues we face and new strength to help us heal.

Five years ago if you had walked into a bookstore and asked for a book on growing up as the child of an alcoholic, chances are the clerk would have given you a puzzled look and you'd have walked away empty-handed. Today there are so many interesting and useful books on the market that there wasn't room to cover them all in the reading list that follows.

As adult children of alcoholics talk, we are coming to learn that healing is an ongoing process; it doesn't end the day we graduate from high school, settle into our own apartment, or even marry and move halfway across the country from our family. It is true that sometimes we feel temporarily stopped or stuck by our past, but history doesn't have to repeat itself. We can learn to grow and to change old thought and behavior patterns. The key to success is to remember that growth toward healing is something we must pursue the rest of our life.

We also are discovering there are more of us than we thought before. Family therapists have found that the patterns of interaction in our families are very similar to those in other families with different problems. The ways of reacting we developed to survive our childhood are shared by people who grew up with emotionally, physically, or sexually abusive parents. They are shared by some people whose parents divorced and even by people who grew up with a parent who worked so hard that he or she was rarely available. Any dysfunctional family, one that doesn't function as it should, has a negative impact on those who grow up in it.

The fact that so many people grow up in dysfunctional families and have problems because of it has caused psychologists and family therapists to take a serious look at the effect our families have on us and to give us new tools for coping. Three major areas of focus during the past five years have been shame, codependency, and inner-child work.

The Shame Game

When human beings do things that are counter to their values, whether they take penny candy from a store or call a good friend a terrible name, they feel guilt. All of us are familiar with the sinking feeling that we've done something wrong. Often guilt is what inspires us to correct our behavior. We pay the store owner and promise ourselves not to take what isn't ours. We apologize to our friend and make a conscious effort not to hurt people with words.

People who grow up in alcoholic homes or in families with other serious problems often experience a poisonous and crippling emotion called shame. Instead of feeling bad about what we've *done*, we feel that *we* are bad and that there's nothing we can do about it. Somehow we're never good enough. we're less than other people, maybe not even fully human.

Our shame can get started in many ways. We may have a parent who repeatedly teases us to the point of tears or one who blows up in anger at our fairly typical teenage behavior. We don't need to hear, "You're no good!" very often when we've neglected to clean our room or to take out the trash before we start believing it—especially when the shaming began when we were very young.

Neglect can cause shame, too. When a parent ignores us or even acts as though we don't exist (as many alcoholic parents do), we may come to believe that we aren't real people. We just don't count. Often while our alcoholic parent is ignoring us, our other parent wants to get too close. Because he or she does not have a healthy relationship with another adult, we become the person to share secrets with, to depend upon emotionally. Those deep, dark secrets add to our already heavy burden of shame.

In alcoholic homes, we quickly learn that we'll be shamed for honestly showing any emotion, so our feelings become tightly tied to shame. When we feel like crying, we are ashamed of that urge and stop ourselves from expressing our pain and sadness. When we are angry we're overcome with shame, and we smile rather than tell others we're displeased with what they're doing. One of the most common defenses against shame is the perfectionism we discussed in Chapter V. Before long our lives become an act, and we're terrified to show other people who we really are for fear they'll hate us and abandon us.

Another common way we try to hide from our feelings of shame is by withdrawing and behaving compulsively. Some of us go on to develop our own addiction in an attempt to dull the pain of our shame. Marcie began collecting *Star Wars* souvenirs when she was in fourth grade. She had never felt that she fit in with the other kids. But the day her mom showed up drunk at school to yell at the teacher was the worst in her life. The kids teased her until she wanted to die.

Her new hobby soon became her escape from shame and eventually from the world. By the time she was a tenth-grader it was her whole life. A virtual hermit, she had no friends and participated in no after-school activities. Beyond homework, her every free hour was spent in poring over her catalogs and working to earn money for more "stuff." She had forgotten the initial shame that had motivated her to start spaced-out, compulsive collecting. Nothing meant anything to her anymore except for new additions to her collection.

Although shame isn't easy to handle alone, we can do some things to start overcoming that paralyzing sense that our place on this planet is a dreadful mistake. In the first place, we can learn that everybody makes mistakes. When other people say or do things they regret, they aren't zapped by a lightning bolt. We won't be either.

When we have trouble accepting ourselves, we can seek acceptance in Alateen groups and from counselors. Many experts believe that since shame is learned in relationships, the only way to unlearn it is in relationships. We need to find people who will listen to us when we are open about what we feel and who will give us understanding. Once we find people with whom we can be ourselves, we can slowly start disclosing our secret feelings of shame. Often when we talk about them, we find they aren't so awful after all.

The Codependency Trap

Because so many of us carry a deep sense of shame and because we have learned to get through life by trying to make other people happy, we may suffer from something called codependency. This addiction to people has its roots in the people-pleasing behavior of the peacemakers we talked about in Chapter V.

Experts at "knowing" what other people need and giving it to them before they have a chance to ask, codependents stop taking care of themselves emotionally. When they feel sad or angry or hurt, they may not even be aware that they have those feelings, let alone can do something about them. Instead they try to feel better by relating to other people, often the first person who happens to come into their life when the negative emotions start to stir.

Because codependents need people who need people, they often choose friendships and love relationships with persons who seem to need fixing. Sam's best friend, John, is a carefree, happy-go-lucky pain in the neck. He borrows money and never pays it back, copies his homework assignments from Sam's papers, and flirts with his girlfriend. Still Sam hangs out with John and can't imagine life without him. When the other kids ask why he remains friends with such a loser, he shrugs his shoulders, but deep inside he's convinced that if he told John to get lost he wouldn't have another friend.

When we're acting codependently, we don't have relationships or friendships; we take hostages. Even though we tell ourselves that we're good, kind, and helping people, we often choose our friends so we can be needed. They aren't independent, so they can't afford to walk away from us. We're secretly terrified of equal relationships where give-and-take occurs. The down side of codependent relationships is that we're always the giver and allow other people to take advantage of us, so we start feeling resentful. We'd rather live constantly with a low-boil anger than cut loose the relationship.

We can start to escape the codependency trap in much the

same way we learn to acknowledge our shame—by accepting ourselves as we are and by practicing healthy ways to relate to people in the safe environment of a self-help group or a counseling relationship. Rather than looking for love in all the wrong places—always from other people—we need to learn to nurture ourselves.

Working with Our Inner Child

Recently many psychologists and other professional helpers have begun to talk about our inner child, the hurt and scared little boy or girl who is trapped inside of us and who, if ignored, will control our life no matter how cool we try to be on the outside. When we were younger, we learned that our parents didn't accept us as the little kid we were. They often needed us to be older and more responsible. Since when we did this there was no way we could act our age, we learned to pretend to be more mature than we really were.

Even though along the way to being a teenager we managed to do a great deal of physical, mental, and emotional growing, there's that little kid inside. Sometimes the inner child is angry because he or she never got to go to the zoo like other kids and insists on playing even though there's an Algebra test tomorrow and an English essay due. At other times your inner child may feel very frightened of being abandoned, and suddenly *you* feel scared and don't know why. Sadness to the point of depression can be triggered by things that you think should be insignificant, but your inner child doesn't.

Most teenagers and adults are not comfortable acknowledging the existence of an inner child, no matter how real that part is. The truth is that pretending we don't feel our feelings doesn't make them go away. Pretending that a very real part of us doesn't exist doesn't make it vanish.

When we respond to our inner child's stirrings by stuffing

that part of us more deeply inside and trying to ignore it, we abuse it emotionally as much as our alcoholic parent emotionally abused us. When we neglect it, yell at it, or try to beat up or shut up that invisible child, it is ourself we are hurting.

Letting our child out doesn't mean that we start having temper tantrums and crying fits. It doesn't give us an excuse to go through high school like a two-year-old or a four-year-old. It does mean we have a chance to reparent ourselves and to fill in some of the love and learning gaps we missed out on growing up in an alcoholic home— including gentle, loving, and consistent self-discipline.

The answer to healing ourself ultimately lies in accepting ourself as a whole person, inner child and all. We learn to love that scared little boy or girl; to listen to what it has to tell us; we reassure it and care for it no matter what. In the process we move past shame and codependency, learning to love ourself. A happy childhood is something we can never claim once we're no longer children; a happy adulthood is within our grasp if we will reach for it and grow.

APPENDIX A

RESOURCES

Sometimes you may not be able to find help on your own: Local groups aren't listed in the phone book, or your teachers and counselors don't know about the resources available to children of alcoholics. Here are some organizations for you to contact. It may take two or three tries before you find out what you want to know. You might want to ask a group to put you in touch with someone who can help you even if they can't.

Adult Children of Alcoholics
P.O. Box 35623
Los Angeles, CA 90035
 This traditional 12-step group publishes a newsletter and offers recovery groups that can help older teens work through childhood hurts.

Alcoholics Anonymous (A.A.)
General Service Office
P.O. Box 459, Grand Central Station
New York, NY 10163
 They publish literature on alcoholism and can put you in touch with the groups nearest you.

Al-Anon (Alateen)
Family Group Headquarters
P.O. Box 862, Midtown Station
New York, NY 10018
 Al-Anon publishes booklets and books for teens living in alcoholic homes and can refer you to Alateen groups near you.

Community Intervention
220 South Tenth Street
Minneapolis, MN 55403
    This group will work with a teacher, guidance counselor, or interested adult to set up support and peer counseling groups for teens.

National Association of Children of Alcoholics, Inc. (NAOCA)
31706 South Coast Highway
South Laguna, CA 92677
    NAOCA helps children of alcoholics and professionals who work with them. The student membership fee is $1.

National Black Alcoholism Council
310 South Michigan Avenue
Chicago, IL 60604
    This organization can provide information about alcoholism in the black community.

National Clearinghouse for Alcohol Information
P.O. Box 2345
Rockville, MD 20852
    They gather and distribute information about alcohol and alcohol-related topics and will try to answer your questions.

National Council on Alcoholism, Inc. (NCA)
12 West 21st Street
New York, NY 10010
    NCA will tell you what help is available or refer you to your state council on alcoholism for local information.

National Self-Help Clearinghouse
Graduate School and University Center
City University of New York
33 West 42nd Street
New York, NY 10036
    Send a stamped, self-addressed envelope and they will put
    you in touch with the type of self-help group you want or
    with a regional clearinghouse that may be able to help
    you. They also give advice about starting your own self-
    help group.

Students Against Drunk Driving
10812 Ashfield Road
Adelphi, MD, 20783
    You may not be able to stop your parent from driving, but
    this group is a good place to put your energies.

APPENDIX B

FURTHER READING

The children of alcoholic parents movement has grown by leaps and bounds over the past few years. A number of very useful and encouraging books have been written explaining the problems faced by people with alcoholic parents and how to start working through those problems. Some of these books are written primarily for adults but contain positive and easy-to-understand information that teens can put to use in their daily lives. Others are written especially for teen readers. We've starred the books for teenagers, but do explore some of the others.

Codependent No More, by Melody Beattie. Hazelden. If you are a people pleaser and spend most of your time taking care of others emotionally, this is a good book for you.

Days of Healing, Days of Joy, by Earnie Larsen and Carol Larsen Hegarty. Hazelden. A daily meditation book that offers support and helps children of alcoholics make changes in their lives.

Following the Yellow Brick Road: The Adult Child's Journey through OZ, by Joy Miller and Marianne Ripper. Discusses the road to recovery from childhood hurts by using examples from *The Wizard of OZ*.

For Troubled Teens with Problem Parents, by the Bureau of Alcoholic Rehabilitation. Hazelden. Written by teenagers of alcoholic parents, this pamphlet examines teens' feelings about their lives.

Grandchildren of Alcoholics, by Ann Smith. Health Communications. Covers the problems that can occur in families when grandparents are alcoholics even though parents aren't.

Healing the Child Within, by Charles Whitfield. Health Communications. A book that helps to heal the hurt and scared child all children of alcoholics carry around inside of them.

Hope for Young People with Alcoholic Parents, by Ann M. Balcerzak. Hazelden. An elementary and junior high school level pamphlet explaining what happens in alcoholic families.

Learn About Children of Alcoholics. Hazelden. Cartoons make it easy to learn about the myths and realities of living with an alcoholic in this pamphlet.

A Teenager's Guide to Living with an Alcoholic Parent, by Edith Lynn Hornik-Beer. Hazelden Books. Examines situations teenagers encounter living with an alcoholic parent and discusses ways of dealing with feelings.

The Secret Everyone Knows, by Cathleen Brooks. Hazelden/Cork. An honest and moving book about coping with problems and reaching out for help.

Time for Joy, by Ruth Fishel. Health Communications. A joyful book of affirmations that helps the reader make it through one day at a time.

Whiskey's Song, by Mitzi Chandler. Health Communications. The true story of one woman's childhood in an alcoholic home.

With Gentleness, Humor and Love, by Kathleen W. and Jewell E. Health Communications. A workbook to help adult children of alcoholic parents recover through the 12-step process of A.A.

*Young, Sober & Free, by Shelley Marshall. Helps teens deal with their own chemical dependency problems.

If you can't find these books in your library or bookstore, or if you would like to discover more books about growing up with a chemical dependency problem in the home, write the following book publisher/distributors and ask for a free catalog.

HAZELDEN EDUCATIONAL MATERIALS
Pleasant Valley Road
Box 176
Center City, MN 55012

HEALTH COMMUNICATIONS, INC.
Enterprise Center
3201 SW 15th Street
Deerfield Beach, FL 33442

Index

About the Author

Kay Marie Porterfield has an M.A. in counseling and has been writing about addictions and relationships for twelve years. Her articles have appeared in many national magazines, including *Cosmopolitan, Seventeen, Woman, Single Parent,* and *New Age Journal.* Her other books about dysfunctional families and addiction are *Keeping Promises: The Challenge of a Sober Parent* and *Violent Voices: Twelve Steps to Freedom from Emotional Abuse.*

In addition to writing, she has taught middle and high school English. Currently she is a writing instructor at Metropolitan State College and Arapahoe Community College in Denver, where she lives with her teenage son, Dylan, and her cat, Hobbit.

"As a recovering alcoholic with many years of sobriety, I still believe it is very important to get the message of hope and healing to those who are chemically dependent and to their families," she says. "By writing about addiction and about how we can meet its challenges and grow from them, I am able to reach many people who otherwise might not know that chemical dependency isn't the end of the world. When we honestly face the problem and seek help, we are given a chance at a new beginning."

DATE DUE			